WA
The Hum

CW00408522

To Louis, Thanks &
all the best... Here's
too the full restoration
of your Mojo! Peace
+ Love,

Edited, Designed & Produced by Sean Duffield Sean

£1 Of every book sold is donated to Campaign Against Arms Trade (CAAT)

Additional proceeds will go to Community Arts Projects (CAP), a Brighton based Group

ISBN: 9780955581311

Published by Sean Duffield/ Paper Tiger Comix © Paper Tiger Comix 2011
First Edition: Limited to 750 Copies.
Contact: seantiger@googlemail.com

Dedicated to all those people who have fought in, died from, suffered through, and survived war and conflict.
To those who went through hell and managed to find some kind of life afterwards.
To those who lost loved ones through war.
To the victims of concentration camps, torture and all other kinds of dehumanisation, persecution, terror, and loss of human rights.
For those who die and suffer so that greedy and ambitious people can prosper.
Thanks for reminding us of how lucky we are.

For those who practice non-violence, and strive for peace in the face of hatred, ridicule and bloodshed.
Thanks for reminding us of what being human can be.

I'd like to personally dedicate this book to
Mam & Dad,
I love you both very much

SPECIAL THANKS: Paul Gravett, Roger Sabin, War on Want, Tyra Taylor, Harry Flay, Paul Stapleton, Teresa Smith, John Freeman, Fiona Verity, Debbie Payne, Deborah Mathieu, Russell Willis, Andy Vine.

To Cheryl Smith for all your help and support through the toughest times.

To Noelle Barby, for your encouragement and belief in what i was doing, and for being the kind and thoughtful person that you are.

To Teresa Smith for putting me in touch and liasing with Mazen Kerbaj, Abu Mahjoob, Joe Sacco and Roger, and for inspiring me with your work.

Many thanks also to Maria Gotch, Paul O Connell, Lawrence Elwick, Andy Luke, David Lloyd, Corinne Pearlman, Warren Pleece, Joe Sacco, Ben Jennings, Yaz Edgeley, Fraser Geesin, Rebecca Soliman, Lizzy Carey, Zoe Swann, Robin Lawley, Sean Creed, Alanna, Alli Hooper, Chris Osmond, Tom at Russell Press, Ross Prentice at copyroom, Chris Daniels for CD mastering, Sally Campbell & all at CAAT.

Thanks to Guerrilla Management, Mush Records, Asphalt Tango, On The Fiddle, Solar Kollektiv & DC comics for permission to use their artists work.

Big thanks to everyone else who donated or contributed to this project, and for making it happen!   Peace, Love & Best Wishes, Sean. xx

4.

CONTRIBUTORS
(SUSPECTED TERRORISTS)

Introduction

Welcome. Thanks for taking an interest in the book. I hope you find it informative, moving, and at times entertaining...It took a while, but it got here in the end.

The sad thing is, when putting together a book about war and surrounding issues, you're never short of material. Indeed, the book has grown considerably since it's inception well over 4 years ago, when I planned a 72 page volume. At 260 pages, this work still feels like the tip of the iceberg; there's a whole terrain which could be explored much more widely, deeper, and more thoroughly.

The idea to create this book, was one born out of frustration. I decided back in late 2006, during the Orwellian 'War of Terror' campaign by Bush & Blair, that I wanted to do *something*. I decided to create a work which debunked Bush's claim that "when we talk about war, we're really talking about peace", and which responded to the propaganda we were being force fed on a daily basis.

The whole 9/11 episode and it's immediate aftermath is where the book started; as those times were the catalyst to it's creation. I hoped the work would then expand into other areas; topically, historically, geographically. Thanks to the contributers, this then became the case.

This book shows the realities of war, whilst also exposing the ulterior motives of the warmongers and the profiteers; whether via serious first hand accounts, a journalistic reportage style, biting satire, or through unique, expressive ways that only comics can explore and provide.

There are examples of those who resist the dark forces of war, campaign for peace and for an end to oppression (sometimes at very great personal risk), and those who rebuild after conflict.

The book provides sympathetic voices from those who are victims of war; including refugees, asylum seekers, child soldiers, victims of torture and rape, and also the regular soldiers, many of whom are haunted and deeply troubled by their experiences and conditioning. It was very important to me for this book to be about the personal and emotional as well as political.

A few strips in this book have seen print before; that is deliberate. they help bind the work together, giving a sense of overall continuity and diversity. The majority of the strips however, were made specifically for this book by the artists involved over a four and a half year period.

Raising money for worthwhile causes was at the heart of the project too. Campaign Against Arms Trade was my main choice; a group whose mission is to restrict, and ultimately end the flow of the global arms trade. Some may scoff at this long term aim as a naïve mission, but no humanitarian campaign was ever successful by being defeatist or accepting the corruption and hypocrisies of the time. There is hope for change in the here and now, especially when increasing numbers of people believe there is something they can do, and act. The arms industry's role and vested interest in war largely avoids scrutiny by the media; it has the support of the governments it fiercely lobbys and has been known to bribe, disregard international laws and act inhumanely. CAAT therefore provide an invaluable service to research and expose the industry's illegal and unethical activities.

Accountability is something in today's global climate which is not a level playing field; rather there is one rule for some, and a total disregard of rules by others. Similarly, mainstream media reflects this hypocrisy and puts a greater value and focus on a human life belonging to one side or culture, and devalues human life on the other. This creates a great sense of injustice and anger in many, which the book attempts to address.

Another modern trait is 'war porn'; the obsession for many with desensitizing killing, fetishising military weaponry, and displaying carnage via media or web, to excite, interest, and create detachment. This perverse pleasure of armchair voyeurism, and the difficulties artists have of combatting this, is commented on beautifully in Oliver Schulze's satirical strip "Stop The War", where the critic of the artist's work is sexually aroused by all he views. 'He just don't get it'.

Vince Packard's cover image to this volume, entitled Fallujah, is the opposite of cold aerial night vision footage, where we see indistinguishable blobs exploding in pretty flashes. His emotional and expressive piece is part homage to Picasso's Guernica, with the context that, like the bombing of that small Spanish town, fallujah was another case of terror meted out on innocent civilians. The Wikileaks documents reveal that cancer levels and birth defects in those who survived Fallujah are worse than Hiroshima, though that is a seldom reported fact. That's why i chose it for the cover; it expresses the horror and human cost of war.

Media tends to show war as spectacle, then move on to the next hot topic. We don't really get to thinking about those left behind when the cameras pull away, or after the bombs and the bullets have stopped. For some, the pain, loss and damage caused by war can continue for the rest of their life.

My own personal view is that the real enemies to humankind are those individuals who knowingly exploit divisions and old wounds between people. Fears, old and new hatreds, and cycles of retaliation are kept going, to benefit those who wish to gain politically or financially.

In the West, we can feel overwhelmed by the world's problems. We get fed a diet of war, conflict, despair, and paranoia, and for many of us, on top of our already stressful lives, it's too much to handle. We want to shut it out, we become cynical and defeatist or tell ourselves it's not our problem. Or we decide we want to try and do something, but give up at the first obstacle. In February 2003 the world saw the largest ever pre-war protests from those against the invasion of Iraq. An estimated 38 million people from every continent took to the streets and made their feelings known. It was unprecedented. Nevertheless our will was ignored.

People expected to be immediately listened to which is unrealistic. When neo-cons, corporate lobbyists and politicians spend a huge amount of time plotting and scheming a whole scale invasion, fabricating reasons to do so, they're not just going to give up at the first hurdle. However, when the public weren't listened to, the majority did not sustain the pressure. With wars like Vietnam for instance, a concerted anti-war movement grew and would not go away, & that was a huge key to the war ending and the troops coming home. Had the larger public against the Iraq war kept up the pressure of taking to the streets, of staging effective events and bombarding their representatives and companies involved with letters (rather than just the committed stalwarts), then who knows what might have happened?

In an era where the US, Britain and it's allies now fight war for the benefits of corporate interests; where the word 'defence' is used to describe invading countries and breaking International law, and wild unfounded allegations are given as a reason to do so, I can't help but be reminded of a quote by George Orwell; "Political language is designed to make lies sound truthful and murder respectable, and to give the appearance of solidity to pure wind."

Indeed, as I write this, our glorious leader David Cameron is blowing much hot air, using the same jaded "we have to liberate those arab people" rhetoric as an excuse to bomb Libya and organise more western friendly regime change. Just as with both previous Gulf wars, our country's lastest fight is presented as gallant and noble, rather than just the latest chapter in the ongoing imperialism of corporations and the power mad. It's deja vu of the worst kind.

In a supposed "time of financial austerity" while we see our public sector destroyed and being opened up to corporations, we're able to somehow launch a full on offensive, - excuse me, 'liberation mission' to the largest oil reserve in Africa. A glance at the MOD's website shows that military spending has in fact increased from £32.6 BILLION in 2007/08 to an estimated £36.9Bn in 2010/11 (which will most likely rise due to this latest foray). And as well as the oil companies and the contractors, let us not forget that other industry which benefits most; the arms trade. Companies such as Britain's largest arms manufacturer BAE systems, have been enjoying huge taxpayer subsidies for years, receiving over £900 million per annum. Yes, war wins again, but it's not over, we can instigate change if we are committed to do so, we can all play a small part, as some of the stories in this volume illustrate; the 'little people' do have the power sometimes.

I'd like to say a huge thank you to everyone who made this project possible - from the artists and musicians who contributed to all those who offered funding and moral support.

Let's hope that love, empathy and common sense can one day drown out the drums of war, and lets celebrate those who experience and survive conflict and manage to find inner peace and meaning in their lives. Despite my own anger, frustration, and anxiety regarding the machinations of war, this work comes from a place of love, peace and hope.

Peace, Shalom, Salaam, Paz, Paix, Frieden, Héping, Mira, Namaste & Love to all.
Sean Duffield 2011

IT'S SEPTEMBER 1999. AS A CARTOONIST AND PUBLISHER, I'M GOING TO THE "SMALL PRESS EXPO", A COMIC CONVENTION IN BETHESDA, NEAR WASHINGTON. I'M TRAVELLING WITH FELLOW CARTOONISTS FROM ONTARIO.

I'M NOT DRIVING, THEY ARE. AND TO KILL TIME AND FORGET MY CRAMPED SPACE, I'M READING A BOOK. AS WE LEAVE CANADA TO ENTER THE STATES, THE RADIO ANNOUNCES A CYCLONE IS MOVING NORTHWARD, PROBABLY PASSING THROUGH WASHINGTON.

AT THAT POINT, I REALISE A STRANGE COINCIDENCE: THE TITLE OF MY BOOK.

AS I BECOME MORE FASCINATED BY THIS SYNCHONICITY, THE CYCLONE HAS BEEN MORPHING INTO A TROPICAL STORM. LESS THREATENING MAYBE, BUT STILL... WE FIGURE THAT WE'LL MEET IT IN NEW YORK.

THE BOOK IS ABOUT THE LIFE OF SCIENTIST JOHN LILLY AND HIS LANGUAGE EXPERIMENTS WITH DOLPHINS. THE CIA IS INVOLVED IN THIS, TRYING TO TURN THE WHOLE THING INTO WEAPONS FOR THEIR IDEOLOGICAL WAR AGAINST COMMUNISM.

BUT, AS WE SEE NEW YORK CITY, THE STORM STOPS. WE ARE EXACTLY IN THE MIDDLE. IT LASTS A FEW MINUTES, AND THE WIND STARTS AGAIN IN THE OTHER DIRECTION.

IT'S A STRANGE COINCIDENCE FOR MY MIND ALREADY FILLED WITH THE CIA'S PARANOID WAR CONSPIRACIES.

EVERY TIME I VISIT THE STATES, I HAVE THIS PARANOIA ABOUT CROSSING THE BORDER. THIS UNEASE ABOUT AMERICA'S MILITARY CULTURE. BUT THAT WAS AT MY LAST VISIT.

ALLO?

THIS TIME, IT'S 2001 AND ONCE AGAIN I'M GOING TO THE SMALL PRESS EXPO. IT'S TODAY THAT I HAVE TO DECIDE IF I'LL TAKE THE TRAIN OR THE PLANE.

IT'S MICHEL.

WHAT'S UP?

IT'S THE END OF THE WORLD! THEY'VE BLOWN UP THE WORLD TRADE CENTER WITH TWO COMMERCIAL PLANES AND A THIRD HAS HIT THE PENTAGON!

I DO NOT SHARE MY FRIEND'S APOCALYPTIC APPREHENSIONS, BUT AS MY GIRLFRIEND AND I WATCH CNN, I SUDDENLY HAVE A FEELING OF DREAD THAT I HAVE NOT FELT SINCE THE GULF WAR.

WHO COULD BE INVISIBLE, UBIQUITOUS AND POWERFUL ENOUGH TO CHALLENGE THE MOST POWERFUL NATION ON EARTH? WHO COULD HATE ENOUGH NOT TO EVEN CARE ABOUT THE CONSEQUENCES OF SUCH AN ACT?

AND WHILE THE SECRET SERVICES TRY TO FIND THIS ENEMY THAT ONLY THEY COULD CREATE, MESMERISED WE WATCH PLANES CRASHING AND CRASHING INTO AN INFINITY OF GIANT TOWERS...

I NO LONGER CARE ABOUT MY TRIP. I DON'T EVEN KNOW IF THE CONVENTION WILL HAPPEN. I JUST KNOW THAT ONCE AGAIN, I'VE AVOIDED THE STORM.

BUT AMERICA IS NO LONGER IN THE CENTER OF THE CYCLONE.

OUR WAR ON TERROR BEGINS WITH AL QAEDA BUT IT DOES NOT END UNTIL EVERY TERRORIST GROUP OF GLOBAL REACH HAS BEEN FOUND, STOPPED AND DEFEATED.

"PAY ANY PRICE, BEAR ANY BURDEN"? THAT'S UNREALISTIC. THAT'S BITIN' OFF MORE THAN WE CAN CHEW. AND HOW WE GONNA **PAY** FOR IT? LET'S CONCENTRATE ON GETTING THE GUYS WHO **HIT** US.

EVERY NATION IN EVERY REGION NOW HAS A DECISION TO MAKE: EITHER YOU ARE WITH US OR YOU ARE WITH THE TERRORISTS.

THAT'S NOT RIGHT! THAT'S TOO EXTREME. SON-OF-A BITCH. HE'S JUST TALKING TOUGH TO IMPRESS THE CHEAP SEATS BUT HE'S GONNA TURN EVERYONE AGAINST US.

OUR RESPONSE INVOLVES FAR MORE THAN INSTANT RETALIATION AND ISOLATED STRIKES. AMERICANS SHOULD NOT EXPECT ONE BATTLE BUT A LENGTHY CAMPAIGN UNLIKE ANOTHER WE HAVE SEEN.

WAR WITHOUT END? THIS ISN'T WHAT WE NEED TO HEAR.

AMERICANS ARE ASKING "WHAT IS EXPECTED OF US"? I ASK YOU TO LIVE YOUR LIVES AND HUG YOUR CHILDREN.

I **DON'T** HAVE A KID ANYMORE, YOU SANCTIMONIOUS **PIECE OF SHIT!**

GREAT HARM HAS BEEN DONE TO US.

BUT NOT TO **YOU!** YOU WERE TOO BUSY RUNNING THE FUCK AWAY!

WE HAVE SUFFERED A GREAT LOSS. AND IN OUR GRIEF AND ANGER WE HAVE FOUND OUR MISSION AND OUR MOMENT.

WHAT'S WITH THIS **REVENGE** SHIT? WE DON'T NEED THIS NOW. WE NEED A WISE LEADER WHO CAN CALM US DOWN AND GIVE US ASSURANCE - NOT GET US ALL STIRRED UP!

STEVE IS ALARMED BY BUSH'S SIMPLE-MINDED BELLICOSITY AND WILLINGNESS TO OFFER ANGRY, UNREALISTIC GOALS TO A GRIEF-STRICKEN NATION.

WE WILL RALLY THE WORLD TO THIS CAUSE. BY OUR EFFORTS, BY OUR COURAGE, WE WILL NOT TIRE, WE WILL NOT FALTER, WE WILL NOT FAIL.

NAOMI AND **KEN** DIDN'T DIE SO THIS MOTHERFUCKER COULD WRAP HIMSELF IN THE FLAG!

...AND HE BEGINS TO SUSPECT THAT IN THE NATION'S GREATEST MOMENT OF WEAKNESS, IT IS NOW BEING MISLED AND MISGUIDED BY A DEMAGOGUE WHO IS CYNICALLY BETRAYING THE TRUST OF THE AMERICAN PEOPLE FOR HIS OWN NARROW AMBITIONS.

I WILL NOT FORGET THE WOUND TO OUR COUNTRY. I WILL NOT RELENT IN WAGING THIS STRUGGLE FOR FREEDOM AND SECURITY FOR THE AMERICAN PEOPLE.

NEITHER WILL I, COWBOY. BUT BETWEEN YOU AND ME, FROM HERE ON OUT I THINK YOU AND I ARE WORKIN' DIFFERENT SIDES OF THE STREET.

THE NEXT DAY STEVE IS CONTACTED BY "90 MINUTES", A FAMOUS NETWORK NEWS MAGAZINE, FOR A SPECIAL LIVE BROADCAST ENTITLED "THE HEROES OF 9/11" BECAUSE OF HIS MAYORAL CITATION FOR HIS RESCUE EFFORTS AND HIS STATUS AS A WAR HERO, THE PRODUCERS THINK HE WOULD MAKE AN IDEAL GUEST.

SURE, I'LL PARTICIPATE

THE FOLLOWING DAY FINDS STEVE IN THE "90 MINUTES" STUDIO, BEING INTERVIEWED LIVE, ONE ON ONE, BY FAMED ANCHORMAN ROGER HAMPTON.

MR. KIRBY, YOU WERE THERE IN THE MIDST OF THE HORROR AND CARNAGE DURING THE ATTACK ON THE WORLD TRADE CENTER. LOOKING BACK NOW, HOW DO YOU FEEL ABOUT THESE EVENTS?

I THINK THERE ARE TOO MANY UNANSWERED QUESTIONS. FOR SOME REASON, IRONCLAD ESTABLISHED PROCEDURES WEREN'T FOLLOWED. AS SOON AS A COMMERCIAL AIRLINER GOES OFF-COURSE, AIR FORCE JETS ARE SUPPOSED TO BE SCRAMBLED IMMEDIATELY TO INTERCEPT IT BUT ON SEPTEMBER 11, IT TOOK 80 MINUTES. HOW COME?

YOU KNOW, THAT **IS** WEIRD.

MR. KIRBY, DON'T YOU...

AND I WANT TO KNOW WHY PRESIDENT BUSH WAS READING STORIES TO SCHOOL CHILDREN IN FLORIDA FOR **TWENTY MINUTES** AFTER HE LEARNED THE SECOND PLANE HIT. WHAT THE HELL WAS THAT MAN **DOING?** NEW YORK HAD JUST BEEN ATTACKED! WHAT WAS ON HIS MIND?

16.

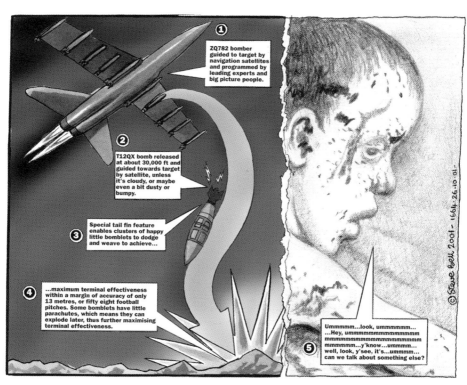

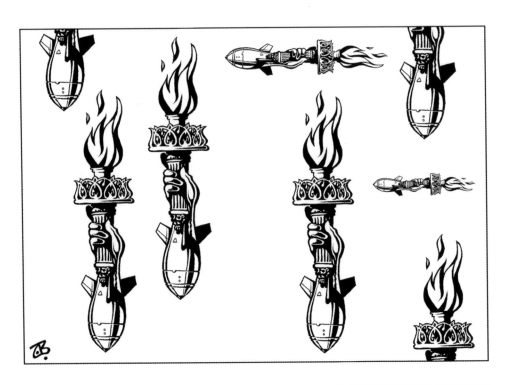

الحرب الامريكية على العراق

21.

HEAL THE WORLD

BY
PIER
GAJEWSKI

05:02

24.

5:11

25.

28.

THERE'S A POWERFUL THIN LINE BETWEEN THE KILLING FIELDS OF AFGHANISTAN AND THE HEART OF YOUR LOCAL JUNKIE...

GROOVY

cultural lethargy

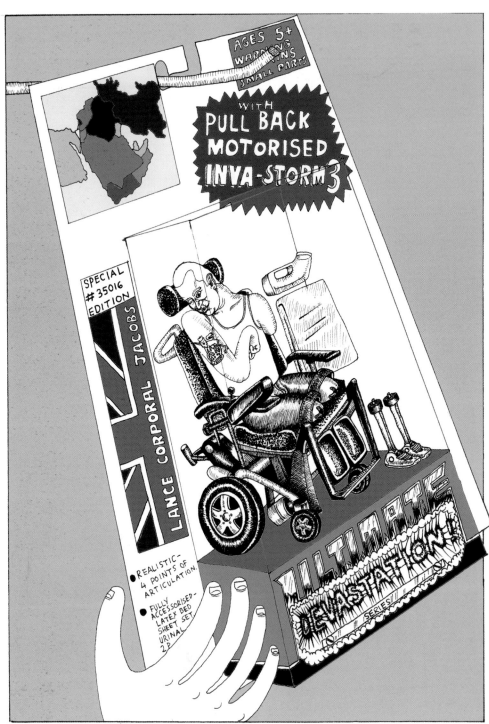

"mummy! mummy! i want this one..."

WAR WOUNDS

BY DEBRA-LYN WILLIAMS
ART BY PEET! CLACK

My Eddie's a good man.
He's served and suffered for his country.
And he's got the scars to prove it.

The day we wed was the happiest of my life.

I cried my heart out the day he went to war.

For three long years he fought in Africa and Italy.

But he never talks about Cassino.

Pinned down by enemy guns, all he could do was watch as the artillery fire crept closer and closer to him.

The screaming shells. The explosions. The howls and shrieks of the wounded and dying.
His hearing's never been the same since.

It was Hell on Earth.

But that was all a long time ago and we live a quiet life these days.
And it's a good life - a happy life.

Except for the nightmares.

He thinks he's back there. In the war.
Fighting for his life... lashing out...

My Eddie's a good man.
Really, he is.

VALLEY DE LOS CAIDOS

GULP

Based on a true story

earlier...

Boy am I glad it's Sunday! Been looking forward to this trip for ages!!

STRETCH

DON'T GO TO THE VALLEY OF THE FALLEN

But what was it Arturo warned me about?

Una ida y vuelta al valle de los caidos*

RAUL

*'Return to the valley of the fallen'

It wasn't until I got off the bus that the penny dropped. Row after row of my "fellow passengers were sporting the same, bizarre uniform: bomber jackets, drainpipe jeans, black t-shirts, shaved heads, and to cap it all off:

steel toe-capped "Bovver Boots"

HOSTIA!*

* "HOLY CRAP"

Everyone's certainly up for it!

What's with all this folk music, anyway?

The banners were another giveaway: the totemic call to arms of Spain's far-right, in all their anachron-istic glory. Young and old, shaven heads and baldies all gathered together on this ordinary Sunday.

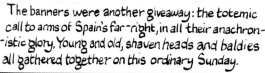

EL GENERALISIMO*

*(the most es-teemed General) Francisco Franco

AKA EL CAUDILLO*

*LITERALLY "THE CHIEF"

Their reason for being there? To pay their respects to...

Appointed Head of State in 1936, Franco led the nationalists against the Republicans in the Spanish Civil War, from which he emerged victorious in 1939. His fascist dictatorship remained in power until his death in 1975.

PRIME MINISTERS NEVILLE CHAMBERLAIN AND LEON BLUM (UK + FRANCE)

SPAIN

Despite the outbreak of war on their doorstep, Euro-pean nations agreed to remain neutral throughout the Civil War (and indeed Franco's brutal reign afterwards).

An estimated 190,000 died in the war.

PICASSO

This didn't, however, prevent Nazi Germany from bombing the Basque Country (Guernica) in 1937.

Looks like a monument to the fallen con-struction workers wouldn't go amiss either!

The Valley of the Fallen houses Franco's grave and basilica and was built by Republican POWs, 14 of whom perished during its 18 year construction.

Setting aside the irony of the world's largest crucifix being built on fascist foundations, the cross is symbolic of the unholy alliance between Franco and the Catholic Church—in 1960, Pope John XXIII declared the crypt a basilica. The dimensions are actually larger than those of St. Peter's, Rome.

AGAIN??

Forgive me Father, for I have sinned...

Franco's oft-quoted aim was "to equal the grandeur of the monuments of old, which defy time and for-get fulness" and at nearly 500m (150m) tall, it's hard not to be awed, re-gardless of the bigoted arrogance behind it. But surely this can't be a normal turn-Sun- out for a day?

38.

Right-wing literature is everywhere, full of nationalist articles on Spanish unity.

It was only after flipping through the magazine that it dawned on me: Nov 20 was not only the anniversary of both Franco and de Rivera's* deaths, but also the foundation of the Spanish Fascist Party. Hatrick!!

They're not here just to honour the past...

...More, seek solace for the future.

In nomine Patris et filii et Spiritus Sancti

And what better salvation than by hand? The pure white cassocks jar against black.

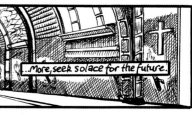

Two uniforms of a sort, with mutually exclu-sive ideologies (or so I had thought)

But even the young'uns swallowed it.

Amidst this tide of idolising devotion, you can see why.

Here, loyalty, pride and glory are exalted above all. Even Jesus seems to have taken a back seat to the Caudillo.

As I made my way back to the welcome centre, I couldn't help but imagine what would happen if word got out that a jew was in their midst.

¿Hueles algo*?

*YOU SMELL SOMETHING?

39.

Would they turn on me as Franco did? The idea of my inherited iden-tity posing a threat was completely alien to me as a liberally raised reform jew from south London.

I played along instead, blending into the crowd in a vain attempt to hide my disbelief at this marching anachronism. (I drew the line at joining in with the singing though)

toda por la patria española

Or was it? It reminded me of an ex-flatmate of mine from Madrid, 'Petas' (spliffs)* whose flirtation with the far right fascinated me.

Heh-loh Dan-ee

*3 GUESSES WHERE THE NAME CAME FROM

He'd spent his teenage years as a total Mod—an obsessive for 60s Britain, down to the Vespa and Parka combo.

Aim a chain-jing man, jess?

PUTT PUTT PUTT

This then led to an appreciation for Blaxploitation, Funk 45s and old school RnB. He turned black overnight.

Git up Git on up-ah

When I next saw him, only a year later, it was quite a different story. This time, he boasted of his exploits at an Atlético Madrid match.

He'd fallen in with 'los ultras', a group of right wing skinheads that evolved from football hooligans who supported Atletico. They were reknowned for their brutal and indiscriminate violence.

Petas revelled in the controversy this brought his way.

His audience's predictable disapproval only exacerbated his urge to be diff-erent, prompting him to showcase all of his right wing paraphenalia: comics, white power tapes, even his email.

EL JUDIO!

ACTUAL COMIC STRIP INVOLVING A FASCIST PINUP HEROINE WHO SEDUCES EVIL JEWISH MEN THEN LURES THEM TO THEIR DEATH

The more time I spent with him the second time round, the more un-comfortable I felt. And yet he openly acknowledged my Jew-ish roots, as did I...

Eet is my only Jewish friend!

...albeit mainly for comic effect

* staysssharp@hotmail.com for all fanmail

40.

Petas' adolescent quest for an identity was one thing, but back at the centre's café, the family-based clientele was quite another.

Franco's familial appeal was evident in 2006 when a far-right Polish Member of the European Parliament expressed admiration for el Caudillo:

He guaranteed the maintenance of traditional values in Europe!!

ALL ROUND NICE GUY MACIEJ GIERTYCH

Thankfully, few shared this opinion, and the last statue of el Generalísimo in Madrid was pulled down in 2005.

Talk about Operation "Enduring Repression"!

Soon after, in March 2006, a unanimous European Parliament "firmly condemned" the "multiple and serious" human rights abuses committed under Franco from 1939 to 1975.

Where are we up to again?

Only 32 more years til we're up to date!

1975.

Incredibly, this was the first official condemnation of Francoist repression. More incredible still is the fact that the majority of Francoist archives remain inaccessible to the public.

José Luis Rodríguez Zapatero's PSOE* victory in the 2004 election has accelerated the process of unearthing the past, but many fear the re-opening of old wounds.

* SPANISH SOCIALIST WORKERS PARTY

The Law on the Historical Memory of Spain was approved on 28 July 2006 but is still yet to be voted, over a year later.

The authorities have been urged to set up an underground exhibition

In the Valle de los Caídos monument

To finally explain the terrible history of its construction

and at last pay heed to the fallen forgotten by history.

© ARCH '07

AN AK47 TALE by ben naylor

Hello.. my name is Standardised 9mm Ak47 Assault Rifle... Ak47 for Short.

scrap book

This is my dad Mikhail Kalashnikov.

I was born in 1947 in a factory in Russia. I weighed 3·8kg when empty and 4·3kg when loaded with ammo.

Очень приятно

I was a precocious little scamp and was being issued in large numbers to Soviet troops in 1956.

My work takes me all over the world. You name a place and I've been there.

Los Angeles
Kazakhstan
Afghanistan
Mexico
Vietnam
Columbia
Somalia
Chile
Rwanda

I Pride myself on being very user friendly..

I could always turn up and get along with anyone I met..

Kids love me.

However as time went on things changed. I started to question my role in the world. Unfortunately not many other career options are open to you when your main selling point is your ability to provide an excellent and reliable rate of fire.

So Mr 47... Why do you think you would be suitable for this teaching position?

I can spit out 600 rounds of ammo per minute with an effective range of 300 metres.

Right. Well thanks for coming.

I got quite a lot of film work in the 80's..(this is me with Sly Stallone at a Planet Hollywood opening)..But apart from that its been business as usual.

PLANET HOLLYWOOD

Also its next to impossible to keep track of all my children... I have 1,000,000 illigitimate kids being produced each year.

Did you know Im on the flag of Mozambique? Also the coat of arms of East Timor, the flag of Hezbollah and the logo of the Iranian Islamic Revolutionary Guard... I didnt ask to be. Maybe something else will turn up but with the state the world is in,

Im not too optimistic...

BANG! BANG!...

Private Military and Security Companies (PMSCs) sell security and military services around the world. These mercenary groups have brushed up their image and moved into the corporate boardroom, becoming a 'normal' part of the military sector. The PMSC industry comprises hundreds of companies operating in more than fifty countries worldwide. They have grown exponentially in recent years due to the occupation of Iraq, which has allowed British mercenaries to reap huge profits. This has allowed the British PMSC sector to grow into a multi-billion dollar industry.

The UK government has failed to enact laws to punish their human rights abuses. No prosecutions have followed hundreds of accounts of personnel from private military and security firms committing abuses in Iraq.

A website run by a former employee of the UK-based Aegis Defence Services showed security guards randomly shooting automatic rifles at civilian cars. Aegis is led by Lieutenant-Colonel Tim Spicer, who broke a UN arms embargo on Sierra Leone with his former company Sandline International, and was jailed in Papua New Guinea for earlier activities.

Human rights abuses by private military companies' personnel have also included torture, rape, humiliation and using dogs to terrify prisoners in the Abu Ghraib prison in Iraq, as well as earlier involvement in rape and prostitution rings in Bosnia. Tough legislation is needed as a matter of urgency to ban the use of mercenaries in these conflict situations.

Caging The Snow Lion Introduction

I first discovered Palden Gyatso when i read an interview with him in Peace Magazine several years ago. I was horrified by his ordeals, and astounded by his resilience and spirituality in the face of 33 years of incarceration and brutal torture by the Chinese regime. He remained unbroken, unwilling to accept that Tibet was owned by China, and adamant that he would not denounce his beloved teacher, the Dalai Lama.

After reading this extraordinary article of a man who can also find compassion for those who tortured his fellow Tibetans and murdered his family and friends, I decided to discover more about the past and current situation in Tibet, and about Palden himself. The following strip is based on over 2 years of research from many sources including aid and humanitarian groups, documentaries, books and moving first hand accounts of Tibetan nuns who I saw at a rally in London. These nuns were survivors of torture in prison and they sung to us one of their beautiful songs, which they created to help them get through such a dark time.

The core influences however are the brilliant documentary "Tibet: Cry Of The Snow Lion", and Palden's book; "Fire In The Snow" which i highly recommend to everyone, as it is such a gripping and enlightening read. It was primarily his book which inspired this strip, and I've stayed as true to Palden's own words and experiences as possible, although I have had to omit much due to space and time restrictions.

I am conscious that the strip does not show the occupying Chinese forces in a favourable light, but it is not meant to be anti-Chinese, rather critical of the occupying regime. Having read about Palden's experiences, I realise there were occasions when one or two guards would show him kindness when noone else was around, but this was a rare occurrence. The reality is, Mao's regime (and to a slightly lesser degree, his successors), dictated that any kindness or sympathy shown to 'reactionary enemies of the people' or 'splittists' (the term given to those who disputed the Communist Party's claims that Tibet is a part of China) was akin to supporting them. This would be met with severe punishment and/ or imprisonment; it was a great risk for soldiers, guards and their superiors to show kindness and compassion, so this seldom happened, but there were notable exceptions, and those people who did were very brave indeed.

Also, millions of Chinese people suffered greatly through the Cultural revolution, with 30 million Chinese people dying, just as around 1 million Tibetans died through this period from the initial invasion. Both Palden and the Dalai Lama have commented on this and shown they have compassion for Chinese people, but the CCP authorities continue to accuse them of being anti-Chinese and of being terrorists.

What I also could not really bring home in these limited 13 pages, is just how effectively the CCP created fear in Tibetans; how they segregated communities that once lived in relative peace and turned people against one another, by force and through indoctrination. Palden's book really does however bring this home, along with the strength and character of the many Tibetans who resisted.

The last 25 years to present in Tibet

There is also a lot of important information on modern Tibet which didn't make it into the strip, so i'll touch upon it here. In 1987, the Dalai Lama proposed the Five-Point Peace Plan to restore human rights and democratic freedoms in Tibet; a concrete negotiation package with China.
The first point called for the transforming Tibet into a non-violent 'peace zone' to inspire the world and ease tensions between China and it's neighbours by acting as a buffer zone .

The Dalai Lama proposed that China could handle Tibet's foreign affairs and run it's army from inside Tibet, for defence purposes only.

The second point called for the abandonment of China's population transfer policy, which threatens the very existence of the Tibetans as a people. Chinese people are forcibly encouraged to move to Tibet, where they pay less taxes and live cheaper than they did in China. Over 7 million Chinese settlers have migrated to Tibet so far and are continuing to enter, outnumbering the indigenous Tibetan population of 6 million. This figure does not include the 400,000 soldiers and police also in Tibet. The capital of Lhasa has seen most Tibetan homes demolished and replaced by Chinese ones. Three quarters of Lhasa's population is now Chinese, and almost Two thirds of the businesses are Chinese owned.

The third point called for 'respect for the Tibetan peoples fundamental human rights and democratic freedoms'. To this day, Tibetans will be imprisoned for reading the teachings of, or owning a photograph of the Dalai Lama. Tibetans can rarely get jobs if they do not speak Mandarin. Many Tibetans live as vagrants, and so many Chinese view them as backwards and dirty, and have prejudices towards them, even though the system deprives them of equal rights. As for the monasteries, in the last 8 years, over 19,500 monks have been forced from monasteries which are under heavy surveillance. New monks will only be added via strict approval of the Chinese authorities.
Worse still, in 1995, the 6 year old Panchen lama (who traditionally in Tibetan culture finds the next Dalai Lama) was abducted along with his parents by the Chinese authorities and has never been seen again. Amnesty International has asked for proof that the boy is alive but the Chinese govt have refused. China then created it's own bogus Panchen Lama, a young Chinese boy with atheist communist parents, so China can theoretically now choose the next Dalai Lama. Even more alarming is the widespread forced accounts of sterilisation and forced abortions of Tibetan women, which the Chinese authorities claim are untrue, but aid agencies and NGOs are not allowed in to investigate further. Tibetans who are desperate to leave Tibet are shot at and often killed by Chinese border guards. The most famous instance of this was filmed by Western climbers as they witnessed at least 2 people being shot dead, one of whom was a girl who the climbers witnessed being thrown into a hole. On average around 3000 Tibetans attempt this deadly trip across the himalayas. Many die of cold, or suffer amputations through extreme frostbite. There are over 180,000 Tibetan exiles currently, who have little in way of legal rights.

The fourth point was 'restoration of and protection of Tibet's natural environment' and abandonment of China's use of Tibet for the production of nuclear weapons and dumping of nuclear waste. The once beautiful Tibet is being destroyed at an alarming rate to fuel Chinese industry and export markets. Huge areas of Tibet have been deforested, and many nomads have been rounded up from the plains and put into tiny, prison-like walled complexes where they are constantly monitored, whilst Chinese companies dig up the rich minerals, ores and oil.

Point 5: 'Commencement of earnest negotiations on the future status of Tibet and of relations between the Tibetan and Chinese people'. The Chinese authorities continue to create propaganda saying the Tibetan government in exile are terrorists, and accusing the Dalai Lama of inciting riots in Tibet and refuse to negotiate, rejecting negotitions. The UN and International community do very little to help, mostly due to the very lucrative corporate deals the west enjoys with China. Any Tibetans attempting to return to their country are arrested as political prisoners and held indefinately. There are currently over 1000 Tibetan political prisoners in labour camps.

Check out: "Dispatches: Undercover In Tibet" &"Tibet: Beyond Fear". You can watch "Cry of the Snow Lion" here: http://www.youtube.com/watch?v=YsiEIuJFsO8

CAGING THE SNOW LION

BY SEAN DUFFIELD & LAWRENCE ELWICK

My name is Palden Gyatso. This is my story...and Tibet's story.

The Tibet of my youth had it's own culture, language, and customs... Our flag contains an image of the Snow Lion, an ancient magical and spiritual creature of Tibetan folklore.... The Snow Lion represents energy, beauty and dignity.

These qualities are expressed throughout our colourful & playful dance, theatre, music and art, aswell as being elements of our spirituality.

Our current Dalai Lama, Tibet's holy leader & voice of compassion, was born of a poor peasant family. Being aware of inequality, he planned to create change & reform once he had completed his spiritual training as a monk... However before that could happen, China started invading Tibet.

Because of this, he was enthroned prematurely at only 16 years old... One of the first actions of his holiness was to release all of Tibet's prisoners.

Our lives changed greatly in 1950. The CCP's Peoples Liberation Army defeated our own small army & continued into Tibet. I had been a monk for 9 years, I was only 19 ... we did not know what was happening.

At first the chinese soldiers seemed friendly & kind, They said they were peacefully liberating us from imperialism & religion...we did not know what they meant...In our culture one can only liberate oneself.

They gave money to monks, lectured us on com--munism, & helped the peasants to work the land.

But after a while, things changed. The CCP forced Tibetan delegates to sign an agenda giving land to China.

The Dalai Lama refused to sign, nevertheless, China claimed huge areas of Western Tibet as its own, and occupied central Tibet.

In 1954, his holiness was called to Beijing by chairman Mao. The Dalai Lama was impressed by the modernism of China, and the idea of creating equality through economic and social change.
He hoped that he could work with Mao to make Tibet a more modern and equal society, whilst keeping its spiritual identity, but on the last day of his visit Mao told him:

Religion is poison

China continued taking land and "redistributing" it, supposedly to the poor people of Tibet.

Land wasn't taken from just aristocracy however, they were taking land and possessions from others, including those regular people who wouldn't co-operate in the Amdo & Kham regions.

When they got to the land owned by the monks which Tibetans worked, the monks would not leave the monasteries, which led to the soldiers publicly humiliating them.

They viewed we monks as parasites. They would urinate and defecate on us, beat us and try & make the monks and nuns fornicate in the streets, whilst denouncing the Dalai Lama.

Regular Tibetans and monks alike were offended by this, most us were loyal to the Dalai Lama and each other, and didn't appreciate having our own people, religion & culture attacked and abused.

A resistance grew... some monks took to the streets with protests, other people joined an armed resistance, many monks gave up their vows and took up arms to protect their country and the Dalai Lama.

The Chinese became more aggressive...anyone who said Tibet did not belong to China was either killed or arrested and given sentences of up to 25 years without trial. And those sentences could easily grow...

By 1959, things had got very bad. The Chinese req-uested the presence of the Dalai Lama at their military garrison. He was told to arrive without guards. People in Lhasa felt there was a real danger that he would be assassinated, so many Tibetans surrounded his palace & pleaded with him not to go, & others demonstrated. The Chinese started shelling and firing at the crowds.

Around 1000 Tibetans were massacred. To stop further bloodshed, his holiness left Tibet.

I was arrested for being at the palace demonstrations, I was 28. My first prison was sharing a room for 3 or 4 months with so many others we could not move. We were lying in rows, our hands and feet were shackled to each other.

There were no beds, or toilets. Lice were crawling around everywhere. Many of those there had been arrested simply for being in Lhasa at the time.

We were then moved to other jails. My next one had a mattress and a rug in it...At least here we were taken to urinate periodically. People were continuing to be arrested off the streets and there was no room in any of the prisons. It was terrifying.

We were given one small bowl of watery barley soup per day, which was not enough to live on, because they made us work. Many died of starvation and illness.

In the day they would make us pull ploughs like beasts for nine hours a day.

Those who couldn't pull them were lashed with metal whips.

Several of the prisoners were very old. When someone would collapse, the soldiers would carry them away and bury them nearby.

I remember that sometimes, the people were still alive. They would look at us as they were being carried off. We would often cry at times like this.

I was sentenced to 7 years as a 'reactionary'. They'd try to get me to confess to being an enemy of the people, but I didn't see this as true. I was loyal to my people, and our ways. When I expressed this to my captors, I was beaten and told to denounce the Dalai Lama and to say that Tibet was a part of China.

I refused... They then accused me of wanting to bring down the 'People's Republic'. I was beaten repeatedly with fists, sticks and rifle butts for not confessing.

If I were to account all the beatings, interrogations, torture and deaths I saw and experienced over the years in prison, it would fill this entire book and continue into other volumes.
I can only give an insight here.
Hopefully this will move you enough to dig deeper.

At the new prison we were escorted out in teams to construct roads and buildings. Food was scarce, work was hard. All we received from the chinese here was black tea. We boiled the leather from our shoes to make thick porridge to eat. Some boiled grass in water and got ill.

Many more died of starvation. We were not allowed to say that however as it made the communist party look bad. Instead when someone died we said "The breath left him"

Coming up to the third year of my sentence, I managed to remove bricks from my cell wall and escape at night with six other prisoners. We thought it better to die trying to escape than to die in prison.

We travelled across the mountains for five days. On the last day we only had to cross a small pass to reach safety over the Bhutan border. unfortunately, at the same time, a group of soldiers on horses spotted us, we ran in terror and they fired their rifles.

I was hit with a rifle butt to the head. As I fell to the ground, stunned & unable to hear out of one ear, I saw my fellow prisoners being caught and roughly tied up.

We were then taken back to prison. My spirits were low, we had been so close to freedom.

when we got back, the guards and officials made the other prisoners shout at us and call for our execution. This was called a Thamzing session. That night we had to sleep outside in the freezing cold with no bedding.

The cuffs dug into our wrists and ankles. We lie awake wondering if we would be executed in the morning.

We were more useful being worked to death. We were taken to Gyantse, a prison with a much tougher regime. I was sentenced to 8 more years for trying to escape, then shackled with heavy iron cuffs behind my back, and large leg irons with only two chain links between them.

I was receiving special punishment. I couldn't work, I couldn't feed myself, I couldn't even go to the toilet. Thankfully my cellmates were kind and helped me eat, wash and use the buckets. We were given tiny amounts of Tsampa to eat here.

54.

After 7 months, they took of my cuffs. I couldn't move my arms or hands. When I eventually moved my shoulders, terrible pains shot through me. I thought my hands were useless as I still couldn't move them, I panicked.

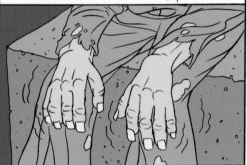

It was 2 weeks before I regained some use of my hands and several months before they were back to normal. My leg-irons remained. In winter they felt like ice glued to the skin.

Every 2 months they would move us all around. It was hard to make friends and sad when you were moved away from people you liked. They did this so we could not conspire or plan to escape. Informers were often placed in your cells.

Simple remarks about the food or any other negative comments remotely connected to the party were reported and guilty parties severely punished. We always got the feeling we were being watched.

In 1964, the Chinese controlled paper 'The Tibet Daily' reported with great indignation, that the Dalai Lama had set up an office in America. We were overjoyed that this support was happening but did not show it. A prisoner called Nyima couldn't contain himself:

Now the most powerful nation in the world is helping us, it won't be long before we are free!".

We knew this was a mistake. Sure enough, his remark was reported by another prisoner. A female guard, a Tibetan called Dolkar, burst in with soldiers and an official and took him from his cell.

Nyima was branded "An evil reactionary bandit" and all our section of the prison were forced to denounce and beat him and call for his execution. Dolkar, the daughter of a Tibetan aristocrat, had contempt for her own people.

She was very ambitious, trying to win points with the officials by getting Nyima to admit guilt. Dolkar got angrier and nastier until Nyima, scared witless and in tears, confessed.

Whilst this was happening another prisoner had vanished, it was presumed he'd escaped. The man was a friendly, popular and jovial monk called Sonam. He worked in the kitchen. He was found behind the kitchen compound later, he had slit his throat with a meat cleaver.

The Chinese decided to blame his suicide on Nyima's 'treachery'.

A week later Nyima took his own life. He had silently stabbed himself in the neck repeatedly with a piece of blunt metal and bled to death whilst in bed.

Dolkar was rewarded with a more powerful position in the women's prison. Many people took their own life due to the abuse and constant fear.

When I felt great pain, mental or physical, I would get angry at them. I once spat at a guard hoping he would kill me to relieve the suffering. I realised this anger was not in tune with my spiritual practice.

I tried to tune out thoughts of anger and revenge. One of the meditations that got me through went like this: 'May I receive it all, may I suffer for all sentient beings, so they won't have to experience this'. My mind was still my own.

We'd get word from the outside world from time to time, from new prisoners. I remember a man who came to trust me telling me about the armed resistance.

The CIA shipped us all to the U.S. for training in guerrilla warfare. Then they sent us back to the mountains with weapons and ammunition.

The U.S. told them they would help liberate Tibet from the Chinese. Although this violence was against my teachings, it gave me hope that things may change in Tibet.

That is until 1972, when a Tibetan official announced that Henry Kissinger was visiting Mao in China and that the USA and China had agreed to do business together.

Nixon came to meet him not long after. U.S. support to the Tibetan resistance ended. Our captors in the prison were ecstatic. They gloated and taunted us. We felt betrayed and depressed by this news.

This was the time of Mao's cultural revolution. A dark time for us all, Chinese and Tibetan. Outside the prisons many Tibetans were beaten and killed by Mao's 'Red Guards'. Monasteries and statues were destroyed and looted, as was anything deemed 'old'. Chinese reformists were locked up with Tibetans too.

We had to burn everything which was not part of the new party. I was even told to burn my new work boots because they were made by 'Indian expansionists'. I didn't know whether to laugh or cry.

People were not allowed to practice their religion. We would be punished for sitting cross legged as it 'emulated buddha'. One time I took a break from work to drink from a stream and splash water on my face. I was reported to have performed the Tibetan ritual of 'water offering'.

I wouldn't confess to this lie. My arms were tied with rope and I was beaten badly daily in Thamzings. The worst beating involved the guards hitting and kicking me for 20 minutes. I couldn't eat solids for over a week.

Simultaneously, a friend I knew, known as Mei Metok, was being given Thamzings for some equally idiotic accusation. One evening, on the way back to our cells, Mei ran out of the line and jumped in front of an army truck. He was killed instantly.

I considered following Mei's example. I felt crushed by the strain of the Thamzings and life in general. My health was poor, I had regular chest pains and couldn't breathe properly. Thankfully on the 13th day the Thamzing stopped. I was told I would be sentenced later.

In the winter I was taken to the "annual assessment", where prisoners deemed to have not reformed were given longer sentences or executed. I was paralysed with fear. Then the guards started dragging in prisoners.

I was relieved I had not been chosen for execution, but repelled by what I knew was going to happen.

I knew two of the men. It's hard to sit and watch someone you know in the moments before their death. My name was read out and I was told to come forward. My heart raced. An old woman was grabbed by the hair, her face pulled up to mine.

She had been beaten terribly and could hardly breathe. I'll never forget her face, it makes me shiver just thinking about her.
Something in her eyes said she was asking for my prayers.

They read out her name and crimes and my heart leaped. It was Kundaling Kusang La. She had led the huge women's demonstration in Lhasa on March 12th 1959.

During her Thamzing beatings she'd kept on declaring Tibet was an independent country.
She was charged as being "a counter-revolutionary guilty of trying to overthrow the motherland".

My brigade leader appeared in front of me.

Palden Gyatso. You are teetering on the edge of a cliff. You are this far from becoming one of these prisoners.

I was so overwhelmed with fear, sorrow and disgust that his words hardly registered.

The guards whipped the prisoners up into chanting "death to the enemies of the people". They were then driven by truck to just outside the prison gates.
We were made to watch.

The officers climbed onto the walkway to get a better view. The prisoners were dragged out one by one and lined in front of a 5 foot ditch.

I felt sick as I watched the prisoners being forced to kneel in front of the trench. The soldiers when ordered, opened fire. The force of the shots flung their bodies back into the trench.

The soldiers then went in close and finished off those who weren't killed by the first volley.
15 Tibetans were shot dead that day.

The families were informed of their loved ones' execution by receiving an invoice of all the costs incurred, which they would have to pay.

The lists were itemised in full, including the cost of the number of bullets fired and the length of jute rope used to bind and gag them.

People's bravery in the face of torture and death astounded me. In 1975 I was supposed to be released. Instead I was sent to a 'labour reform camp'; another prison under a different name. It was here I met Tseten Wangchuk.

The camp existed to seperate class 'enemies' and provide cheap labour. Each morning 200 of us had to scour the hills, filling buckets with animal dung and human feces to be used as manure. competiton was fierce and often there wasn't enough to go round.

One of those men was Tseten. He'd be an estate manager for some aristocrats, so was labelled 'a lacky of the exploitative classes'. Some prisoners would taunt him, so one day he snapped back:

What a wonderful world we live in. We collect shit as if it were precious cake

He was subjected to a brutal Thamzing for 'defaming socialism'. This didn't break his will.

The following morning he wouldn't get up. We pleaded with him but he was adamant. The brigade leader ordered him up and Tseten said "There's no shit in the hills". The brigade leader told him to be more resourceful and look by the roads ... Tseten defiantly replied:

I didn't know trucks could shit. socialist trucks must be superior to capitalist ones!

Work was cancelled. Instead we all had to denounce him. He was abused, beaten then executed.

During my time there children started appearing at the main gate. One of the boys squeezed through and came to talk to me.

Please... My family and friends have not eaten for days

we had been told that outside prison, hunger and food shortages were a thing of the past. But these children were as malnourished as the people in my worst periods of prison.

Beggars in the old feudal society weren't like this, they walked on full stomachs. what was worse is these children were from the poor classes, the people the Chinese claimed to be looking after most.

This famine wasn't about crop failure; they had to surrender the majority of their food to the CCP and pay taxes. Their livestock had been confiscated too. I gave them some of my rations. They became regular visitors.

1976 was an eventful year. I was visited by Nangma, a woman from my village of Panam, who moved to the area to work and who heard I was at the camp.
She told me about my family who had been targeted as members of the 'exploitative classes'.

My stepmother had been paralysed down one side after being brutally beaten by the young Tibetans who had joined Mao's Red Guard.

My older brother who I loved very much had been killed during a Thamzing in 1968. During the cultural revolution my sisters had denounced my father and watched as he was beaten to death by Chinese soldiers.
My step-mother would not speak to my sisters after that.

I wept uncontrollably. Not only had the communists killed and maimed those I loved, they'd managed to divide us too.

There was another significant death for me that year, that of chairman Mao. After his death things eased up a little for a time. We were now being lectured constantly on 'the dawn of a new age'.

Mao's little red books were burned. Atrocities were blamed on Mao and the 'Gang of Four'. Tibetans in the towns were allowed to dress in their own clothes again.
We were told we'd have religious freedom.
The Chinese had begun the 'softly softly' approach.

It wasn't until 1983 that I was released from the camp. I went back to Drepung, one of the few monasteries which had not been destroyed. It was now reopened but had been vandalised, looted and daubed with revolutionary slogans.

Monastic life was now a farce. We were made to wear blue uniforms and forced to work hard for the party. We were only allowed to meet and perform prayers three times a month.
Having pictures of the Dalai Lama was still banned and just as punishable as before. Nevertheless I was glad to be back.

I had been allowed to go to Lhasa briefly at the weekends. I made posters in secrecy which called for independence, stating that the new reforms were just window dressing. I would smuggle them out and put them up near the monastery walls at night.

I knew that this was very risky, but I felt I had to fight the oppression and tell the truth.

Two months after my release, police appeared in the area asking questions. One night they burst in with guns.
My room was ransacked.

My heart sank when tracing paper with the poster heading on it fell out of a book. I was foolish to have kept it. They also found a flag I had hidden and teachings of the Dalai Lama...
...once again I felt tight cold rings of metal forced against my wrists.

I had been out of jail for 3 months and 18 days, and now I was back. That night, I cried myself to sleep.

In 1984, aged 51, I was sentenced to 8 years in Drapchi prison. People sent here were deemed 'unreformable'. The guards were dressed for battle. They each had a pistol, two knives, and two kinds of electric batons.

It wasn't long before I received my 'initiation'. One morning I complained to the cook that our tea was cold. Soon after a guard called Jampa stormed in. He grabbed me, poured scalding water over my arm and said:

I want to test if the tea is still cold.

The water blistered my bare skin. Jampa then prodded me repeatedly with his electric baton, sending shocks through my chest & shoulder.

I was put into a dorm of segregated political prisoners. For the first time, I felt complete solidarity with my cell-mates, & this created an atmosphere of strength & resistance in us.

Outside in Lhasa, resistance was growing too. In 1987, Yulu Tsering, a lama, was arrested for giving an interview with an Italian visitor who filmed him. He was accused of 'spreading counter-revolutionary propaganda'. His arrest sparked protests by the new generation of monks.

Protests continued. Regular Tibetans including children, joined the monks. The CCP became more brutal & in 1989 things boiled over into rioting.
Soon after, trucks brought new prisoners, mostly young boys and girls under the age of 20.

These kids seemed fearless. Many had grown up during the violence & indoctrination of the cultural revolution, but had still rejected the party. Their spirits cheered me greatly and gave me hope. One of those kids was Pemba.

Pemba was a friendly illiterate boy, who asked me to teach him to read and write. I obliged, he was a quick learner, hungry for knowledge.

One of the newcomers dared to write 'Freedom For Tibet' on a prison wall. Pemba was blamed, & I was suspected of coaxing him. Pemba was taken away, never to be seen again.

I was tortured by a sadistic chain smoking guard called Paljor whilst 2 guards watched. He cut my tongue with a knife then repeatedly rammed his electric baton in & out of my mouth. Three of my teeth were immediately knocked out. The pain was unbearable.

He shocked me with his longer baton too. I passed out & awoke in a pool of my own urine and vomit. One of the guards pulled out my tongue to stop me choking, the other ran out in disgust. Later, my other teeth fell out.
I could not eat solids for weeks.

The electric batons were used in women's dorms too. The nuns were told to strip naked, the electric cattle prods were rammed inside their vaginas. Some of the nuns died from this barbarity.

Many of the nuns created songs in prison, & would sing them together to lift their spirits, when the guards were not around. I heard one once. It was so beautiful & sad that it moved me to tears.

This treatment made us more determined to resist. We smuggled messages outside, Tibetans would go up to foreign tourists thrusting the messages into their hands, with instructions to take them to the U.N or their own governments.

In spring 1991, a foreign delegation was coming to inspect the prison. Suddenly fresh fruit, veg and meat appeared in the kitchen. We were given new uniforms. The prison was decorated in brighter colours. We decided to make a petition which described the torture and reality of prison life.

Two of our group said they were ill, & got permission to leave the dorm & see the doctor. Guard duty was relaxed due to the visit, & one of the men, Tengpa, rushed up to the U.S ambassador to hand over the petition, but it was snatched by a Chinese aide.

The two were put into isolation after the visit. Concerned for their safety, all the political prisoners decided to sit and protest outside the prison office and shout 'Where are our people?'

Chinese soldiers rushed in and took up position. A policeman pointed a gun threateningly at each of us in turn. We stood up together as one, he then hit one of the young monks across the face with his gun and it fell out of his hand.

We were then rushed by the soldiers. Fear gripped me as I thought they were going to kill us. Some were using the electric batons. They seemed to be targeting the younger prisoners.

A teenage boy called Phurbu, turned to run from the charge, but a soldier thrust his bayonet into the back of his neck, just below his head. He fell, blood spurting from the wound.

Horrified, I stood there in shock. Just then the butt of a rifle hit me in the back, winding me. The older Tibetan guards tried to intervene and get us back to our dorms, but the soldiers dragged the younger prisoners from their cells. One by one they were beaten and put in isolation.

It was a battle of wills. To those who use brute force, there's nothing worse than a victim's refusal to acknowledge their power. Wounds can heal, but if your spirit is broken, everything falls apart.

Belief in our fight for rights and justice kept us going. We'd rather die in our hearts than submit to those that abused us.

Eventually, after 33 years in prison, I was to be released. I was to discover later that this was mostly due to continued pressure by Amnesty International.

Teacher, take good care of yourself.

I was overjoyed to be leaving, but at the same time saddened & moved to be saying goodbye to some of the finest and most brave people I'd met. I prayed they would be ok.

Contacts from the outside warned me that things were bad & that I would be under surveillance. I decided with their help, I would try & escape Tibet. I told the authorities I would go back to my monastery & live out my days as a monk.

So much suffering....

I got to go back to my village & meet my weak, bedridden step-mother. It was an emotional reunion. I couldn't tell her that I was going to escape.

I decided I would take evidence of torture with me. China was saying that there were no political prisoners and no torture in Tibet, so it was important to prove otherwise.

This is for you.

Before I left prison, I told my contact that I knew an old Chinese guard who would get anything for the right price. Sure enough, one night there was a knock on my door, & a young man handed me a hold-all filled with torture equipment.

Next morning, the same young lad arrived & said it was time to leave. This was it! My family thought I was moving to the monastery. I said my goodbyes, trying to hide my sorrow that I wouldn't be returning.

I was taken to a safe-house in Lhasa. I was told the escape plan and given a suit and tie to change into. I had never worn one before.

Early next morning I was taken a couple of miles outside of Lhasa by bike. I breathed in the air & watched the sun starting to rise.

I was dropped off & told to wait for a truck which would take me to the Nepalese border. I stood waiting, wondering how I would explain a hold-all full of weapons of torture if any army or police showed.

The truck appeared. The driver delivered goods regularly to a merchant in Nepal. The Chinese guards at the checkpoints all knew him, so I was ok, but my heart beat fast nonetheless.

Then came the most dangerous part of my journey. I was dropped off at the border town and introduced to my guide, a elderly Nepalese man. We would wait till dead of night then cross the border.

We climbed through a dense, steep forest at the far end of town. It was raining hard, and the going heavy. At dawn we crossed a small rope bridge, & my guide, who spoke no Tibetan turned to me and simply declared:

I was so relieved! The final part of the journey was by motorbike to Kathmandu with a young Sherpa. He took me to the UN High Commission for refugees.

I was given some money and a travel permit to get to India. I left for Delhi by bus. A few days later I was in Dharamsala, home of the exiled Tibetans and the Dalai Lama.

When I arrived I saw dark storm clouds over in the distance where Tibet was. This reminded me of the darkness & suffering I had left behind, & those who still had to endure it.

Not long after my visit I got to meet his holiness. This was something I had dreamed of. I was taken into a very plain room where the Dalai Lama looked like any regular monk. He asked me many questions & I told him my story & he listened intently and seemed very concerned.

You have faced much hardship

I would now have a home in the refugee camp. His holiness told me I should take time to write about my story and those who shared it. But that is not the end of the story...

I travelled to Geneva in 1995 & met people who helped free me. They were very kind. I spoke to the media & had photos taken with the torture equipment I'd smuggled out. Most items bared Chinese insignias & included knives, wrist & thumb cuffs, electric cattle prods & a shock gun.

I gave evidence to the U.N Commission on Human Rights. When I had finished, I saw that the Chinese delegation were actually listening! I wish my fellow prisoners could have been there to see it. The delegates made no reply.

A while later I was accused by a Chinese ambassador of being a criminal guilty of trying to overthrow the government & of theft. He said my testimony was untrue and torture was forbidden.

I continue to protest worldwide. In 2006 I travelled to the Turin Winter Olympics with some young monks & went on hunger strike. We drew attention to the fact that China was hosting the 2008 Olympics, whilst Tibetan people were suffering in terrible conditions.

Oppressors will always deny they are oppressors. When I speak of suffering, I do so for all those Tibetans still in prison and living in fear.

The cruelty has not stopped, despite what you may read or hear. It will go on until Tibet is free, and I hope that day may still come...

Zatchula was a cheerful, clever, beautiful little girl who I befriended in Afghanistan.

I was a soldier there, and I would pass her dollar bills, candy, and little gifts through the constantine wire.

About two thirds of the way through my year in country, I realized that I wouldn't be able to substantially help her, or give her any real opportunity to escape her surroundings.

I get sick to my stomach with guilt when I think of her, and the almost inevitable hardship she will have to face in that unforgiving place.

-Bill

ZATCHULA by front gate '04

THE SOLDIER
story and art: hannes pasqualini

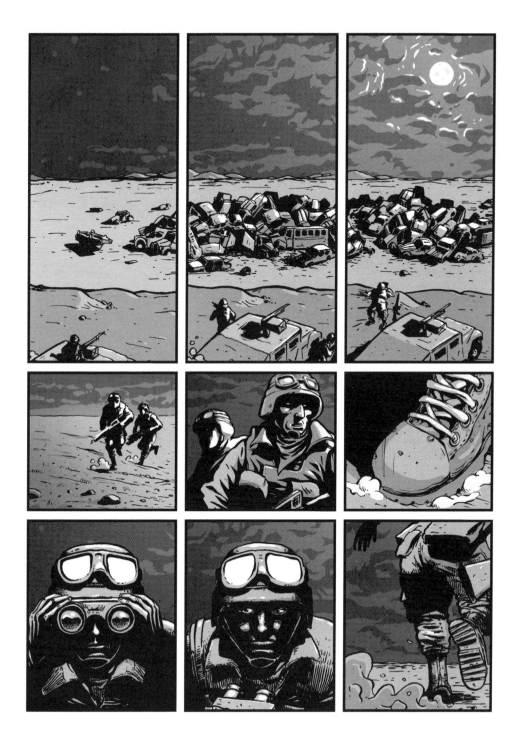

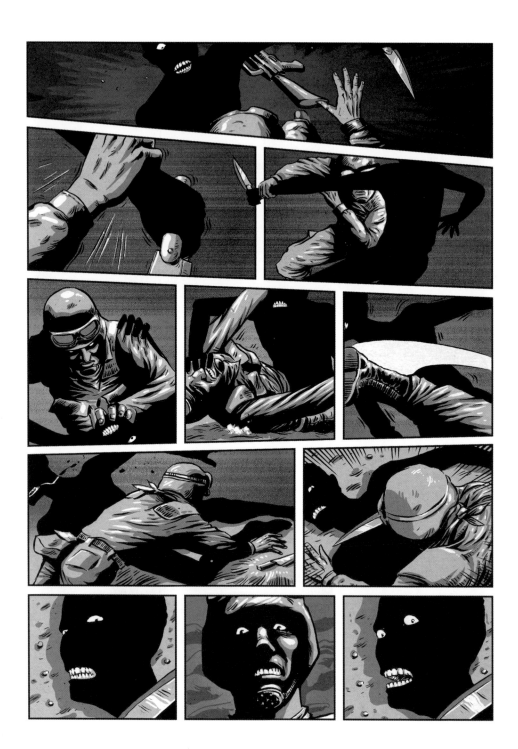

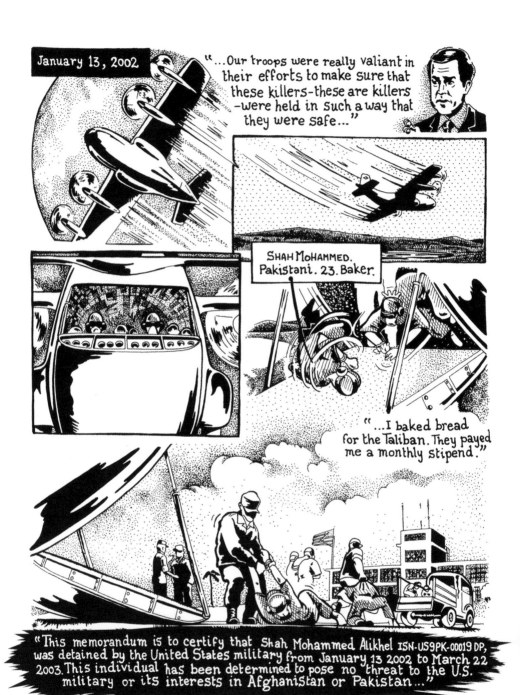

"...There are no charges pending from the U.S. against this individual. The U.S. goverment intends that this person be fully rejoined with his family."

This letter was given to Shah Mohammed when released. He was one of the first prisoners to be taken to:

CAMP X-RAY

GUANTANAMO

a. Alvarez 2004

Sited on the northern side of the U.S. naval base it was named after one of the symbols in the phonetic alphabet used for official military radio communication (ei: Alpha, Bravo, Golf, x-Ray)

keep your head down!!

Originally constructed to hold Haitian refugees in the 1990s, it was now to serve as a holding facility for Al Qaeda, Taliban and other detainees under U.S. control during the war on terror.

The U.S. Southern Command activated Joint Task Force 160 to take care of the captured enemies in Guantanamo.

Told you to keep your head down!!

Asif Iqbal, Briton, 22

We travelled to Pakistan ahead of the marriage my parents arranged for me. He was going to be best man

I hoped to do a computer course after the wedding.

Asif Iqbal, Ruhal Ahmed and Shafiq Rasul after being released, in the sitting room of a suburban House in Tipton, England. Sunday March 14, 2004.

"We were travelling through Afghanistan in a taxi trying to escape to a safer place..."

"...but when we reached Kunduz the city was surrounded by the Northern Alliance Forces."

"One thing made us dangerously visible, we had no beards."

"We were captured and taken through the open desert with thousands of prisoners outside Shebargan prison."

"There they herded us into containers, maybe 300 of us into each one."

"We were suffocating. It got really hot and everyone started screaming and banging."

76.

"We lived because someone made holes with a machine gun, though still more died from the bullets..."

"..I had not drunk for more than two days. We stank, we were covered in blood, urine and the smell of death."

"Freed from the containers we were taken into Shebargan prison. People died daily there..."

"I'll never forget one Arab who was missing half his jaw. For 10 days until his death he was screaming continuously begging to be killed."

"One day we were put in chains, hooded and handed over to the U.S. Special Forces. They took us to Kandahar."

ABDUL RAZAQ
Pakistani. 31.
English teacher.

Many of the people taken to Kandahar and then to Guantanamo Bay were simple bystanders. In an interview, after being released, Abdul Razaq declared:
"I'm convinced that the only reason I was sent to Kandahar was because I spoke English. When a soldier came and asked who among the prisoners spoke English I stepped forward..."

78.

"I don't have the slightest concern about their treatment after what they have done." Defense Secretary, Donald Rumsfeld.

"...In the first one-and-a-half months in Guantanamo they wouldn't let us speak to anyone, there was almost nothing to do. You just stare and the hours go clicking by. You'd look at people and see they'd lost it. There was nothing in their eyes anymore. They didn't talk..."

MOHAMED SAGHIR
Pakistani. 53.
Sawmill owner

*Allahu akbar
Allahu akbar
Allahu akbar
Allahu akbar

"...They wouldn't let us call for prayers or pray in the room..."

* God is most great.

Who is it ?!!

*Ashhadu anna Muhammada-rasulu-llah
Ashhadu anna Muhammada-rasulu-llah
Hayya 'ala-salah Hayya 'ala-salah.

* Ashhadu an la ilaha illa-llah
Ashhadu an la ilaha illa-llah

* I witness that there is no god except God

*I witness that Muhammad is the messenger of God. Come to prayer.

79.

ABDUL RAZAQ

...Where's Osama?

I-I don't know.

Do you know any of the Al-Qaida leaders?

No

Hm...

Where did you say Osama was last time you saw him?

No, I didn't say that...

"I've been questioned between 10 and 20 times."

"Each time the interrogators were different, but questions were the same."

"They asked the same questions several times. A tactic to catch us off guard."

SHAFIQ RASUL

Come on...

He's wasting our time. Just take him to the isolation cell.

Hey, give him another chance

He's going to cooperate

"During the interrogation our chains were fixed to a metal ring in the floor."

"Sometimes they used the good cop / bad cop routine."

"I knew what they were doing. I think they tried it more with some of the Arabs and the young kids"

JAMAL UDEEN

I quite like that...

The music's great

"Once they started playing different music to see how I would react."

"They started with Kris Kristofferson. Then some Fleetwood Mac songs!"

"They didn't play it again."

81.

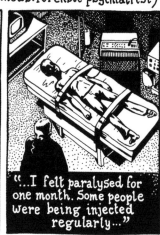

This is civilization's fight. This is the fight of all who believe in progress and pluralism tolerance and freedom.

In April 2002 prisoners were moved to Camp Delta and Camp X-Ray was closed. At that time more than 600 people were held there, including four children.

May, 2003

Here you are.

Shah Mohammed was transported from Cuba back to Pakistan "in chains."

And like Abdul Razaq, Mohammed Saghir, Shafiq Rasul, Asif Iqbal, Ruhal Ahmed and many others was released to go free.

During more than a year he was held without formal charges or access to legal counsel

And so I'm looking at the legalities involved with the Geneva Convention. We are not going to call them prisoners of war. And the reason why is Al-Qaeda is not a known military.

These are killers. These are terrorists.

"They promised me some money but at the end they gave me this bag with a pair of jeans, a shirt and a pack of tissues..."

"These guys get shipped to somebody else's country, held there so they don't get the same rights as in the U.S., and then get treated by rules made up by the government to suit their interests..."

84.

"...If we are trying to say to the rest of the world we have due process and best practice in our country... we shouldn't be treating other people in ways that are unfair." James Harrington. New York lawyer.

The Bush administration's decision is that the few detainees facing trial should stand before a military commission, which would take place without juries or appeal to a higher court but with the power to impose a death sentence.

PAUL WOLFOWITZ Deputy Secretary of Defense and the Commission's Appointing Authority

• The judges for the military commissions are appointed by WOLFOWITZ.

• Any judge can be substituted up to the moment of the verdict by WOLFOWITZ.

• The military prosecutors are chosen by WOLFOWITZ.

• The suspects they charge and the charges they make are determined by WOLFOWITZ.

• All defendants are entitled to a military defense lawyer from a pool chosen by WOLFOWITZ.

• Defendants if convicted can appeal to a panel of three people appointed by WOLFOWITZ, and then the panel sends its recommendation for a final decision to... WoLfOwitz

In June 2003 the U.S. military officials were making preparations for the construction of a "death chamber" in Guantanamo.

The example being set by the U.S. is being used to legitimise repression internationally on an ever-increasing scale.

U.S. Supreme Court

The judges of the Supreme Court started reading in January 2004 the friend-of-the-Court briefs before deciding on the legality of the situation at Guantanamo. Among these documents, there was one signed by 175 British Peers and Members of the Parliament urging them not to abdicate their role as protectors of the rule of law. Another was filed by retired U.S. federal judges and there was even one filed by five uniformed military lawyers, essentially challenging the authority of the President, their Commander-in-Chief

The President's ranch, Crawford, Texas. March 30, 2002. 12:40 PM CST

meanwhile...

Abdul Razaq: released in May 2002 suffering from schizophrenia.

...there needs to be a focused coalition effort in the region against peace...I mean, against terror for peace...

I have no complaints against the Americans or the Afghans and I don't seek any compensation from anyone.

I leave it to God to reward me.

THE ★ END

FOSSIL FUEL
BY NICOLE SCHULMAN

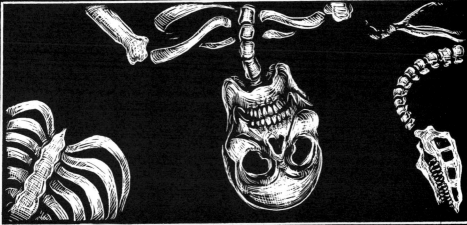

THE BATTALION OF THE VIRGIN MARY

by ulliwel 2007

I REMEMBER THE HORRORS OF MY CHILDHOOD.
IN DARK CORNERS, DEVILS AND EVIL GHOSTS WOULD BE LURKING. STORIES OF KIDNAPPERS AND CANNIBALS WOULD FRIGHTEN ME ENORMOUSLY.

WHEN THE FEAR GRAPPED ME, I WOULD CUDDLE UP TO MY SISTER.

EVI, I CAN'T SLEEP!

BE QUIET ALREADY!

I KNEW THAT OUR MOTHER, BEFORE GOING TO SLEEP HERSELF, WOULD SOMETIMES COME CHECKING ON US.

MOM WILL COME AND COVER ME UP. THEN EVERYTHING WILL BE GOOD.

HALF ASLEEP, I LOVED TO FEEL HER PUTTING THE BLANKET OVER MY SHOULDERS.

CRAC!

PENG

GET UP!

GO!

93.

95.

THE CHILDREN ARE DRIVEN FROM ALL THE HOUSES.

HOURS LATER

WHAT DO THEY WANT FROM US?

WE ARE SUPPOSED TO FIGHT FOR THEM.

I WILL ESCAPE!

IF THEY CATCH YOU, THEY WILL HACK YOU TO PIECES.

HOW WE ARE SUPPOSED TO FIGHT? WE ARE ONLY CHILDREN?!

THEY GIVE US MACHINE GUNS.

WHERE CAN I FLEE TO? DADDY AND MOMMY ARE DEAD. I AM A MURDERER!

MURDERER!

MURDERER!

PENG

MURDERER!

97.

THE VILLAGE I GREW UP, THERE WERE NO WARS, NO EARTHQUAKES, NO TYPHOONS. THERE WAS NO REASON TO BE AFRAID.
BUT I REMEMBER THE FEAR, WHEN IT CAME, WAS OVERPOWERING.

THIS NIGHTMARE WAS, AND STILL IS A REALITY FOR CHILDREN IN UGANDA. THE FEAR THEY HAVE TO LIVE WITH EACH DAY IS UNIMAGINABLE FOR ME.

www.ulliLust.de 2007

FROM 1986 TO 2005, THE UGANDIAN REBEL MOVEMENT LRA KIDNAPPED 30.000 CHILDREN (THIRTY THOUSAND!) TO TURN THEM INTO SOLDIERS — BY THE HERE DESCRIBED METHODS OF »EDUCATION«.

THEIR LEADER, JOSEF KONY, CLAIMS TO BE THE REINCARNATION OF THE VIRGIN MARY.
HE FLED TO THE KONGO WITH 800 REMAINING FIGHTERS IN 2005.
TODAY HE IS CARRYING ON PEACE NEGOTIATIONS.

TODAY THERE ARE APPROXIMATELY 250.000 CHILDSOLDIERS FIGHTING WORLDWIDE.

IN THE KONGO, THEY ARE CALLED »KADAGOS«, IN COLUMBIA »LITTLE BEES« OR »LITTLE ALARM BELLS«, IN LIBERIA THEY ARE FIGHTING UNDER NAMES LIKE »TWO TONS OF TROUBLE« OR »GENERAL LUCIFER«.
SOME ARE HARDLY EIGHT YEARS OLD. THEY ARE THE CHEAPEST AND MOST EASILY CONTROLLABLE CANNON FODDER THE WARLORDS OF THE MODERN WORLD CAN FIND.

www.unicef.org

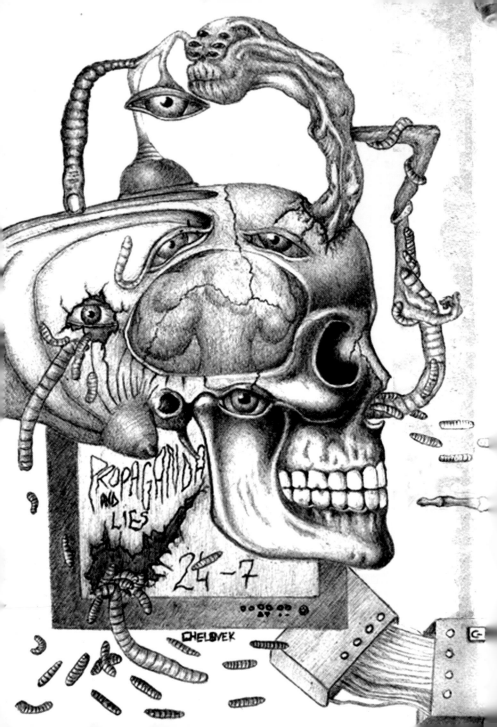

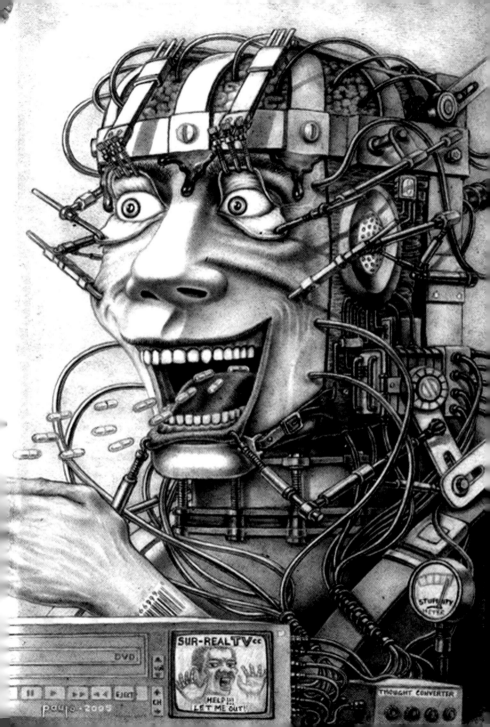

ORWELL ON WAR

NO BOOK IS GENUINELY FREE FROM *POLITICAL BIAS*.

THE OPINION THAT *ART* SHOULD HAVE NOTHING TO DO WITH *POLITICS* IS *ITSELF* A POLITICAL ATTITUDE.

THE WRITER *GEORGE ORWELL* HELD A RANGE OF FAR REACHING *OPINIONS* ON THE SUBJECT OF *WAR*.

HERE LIES ERIC ARTHUR BLAIR BORN JUNE 25th 190? DIED JANUARY ?

ORWELL EXPERIENCED WAR AS BOTH A *PARTICIPANT* AND AN *OBSERVER*...

...AND HIS FEELINGS ABOUT THESE EXPERIENCES SERVED TO UNDERPIN THE REASONS WHY HE CHOSE TO *BE* A WRITER.

IN 1922 *ERIC BLAIR*, BEFORE HE ADOPTED HIS PEN-NAME, WAS *19* YEARS OLD. HIS FAMILY COULD NOT *AFFORD* TO SEND HIM THROUGH UNIVERSITY...

...AND SO WITH LITTLE ENTHUSIASM HE JOINED THE *INDIAN IMPERIAL POLICE* IN BURMA.

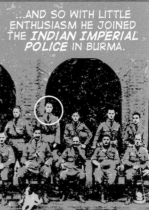

IT WAS DURING HIS TIME WITH THE BRITISH *RAJ* THAT ORWELL REALISED HOW TOTALITARIANISM *DEHUMANISED* NOT JUST THE *OPPRESSED*... ...BUT THE OPPRESSORS *THEMSELVES*.

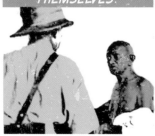

THE TYRANT "MAY *BEGIN* BY WEARING A MASK", SAID ORWELL,

"BUT HIS FACE SOON GROWS TO *FIT* IT."

IN 1927, AFTER 5 YEARS OF SERVICE, ORWELL *LEFT* THE FORCE TO RETURN TO *EUROPE* AS HE COULD NO LONGER *STAND* BEING A "SERVANT OF IMPERIALISM"

IN 1936, AFTER BOUTS OF *ILLNESS* AND *POVERTY*, WRITING AND WORKING VARIOUS JOBS IN *PARIS* AND *LONDON*...

...ORWELL ENLISTED AS A *SOLDIER* TO FIGHT THE RISE OF A FASCIST DICTATORSHIP IN THE *SPANISH CIVIL WAR*.

HE SAW FIRSTHAND THE EFFECTS OF POLITICAL *PROPOGANDA* AND *MISINFINFORMATION* UPON THE COURSE OF THE WAR.

BORN INTO *IMPERIALISM* AND BECOMING SOCIALLY *CONSCIOUS* ALONGSIDE THE RISE OF *FASCISM*...

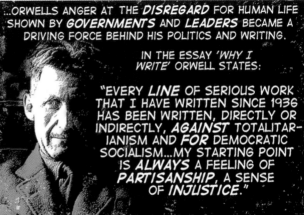

...ORWELLS ANGER AT THE *DISREGARD* FOR HUMAN LIFE SHOWN BY *GOVERNMENTS* AND *LEADERS* BECAME A DRIVING FORCE BEHIND HIS POLITICS AND WRITING.

IN THE ESSAY *'WHY I WRITE'* ORWELL STATES:

"EVERY *LINE* OF SERIOUS WORK THAT I HAVE WRITTEN SINCE 1936 HAS BEEN WRITTEN, DIRECTLY OR INDIRECTLY, *AGAINST* TOTALITARIANISM AND *FOR* DEMOCRATIC SOCIALISM...MY STARTING POINT IS *ALWAYS* A FEELING OF *PARTISANSHIP*, A SENSE OF *INJUSTICE*."

YET AT THE SAME TIME ORWELL ACKNOWLEDGED THE INFLUENCE OF *OTHER* DRIVES IN HIS WRITING, DRIVES SUCH AS *'EGOISM'*.

"TO SEEM *CLEVER*, TO BE TALKED ABOUT, TO BE *REMEMBERED* AFTER DEATH"

ANOTHER DRIVE ORWELL TERMED *"AESTHETIC ENTHUSIASM"*...

ORWELL LOVED LANGUAGE FOR IT'S TEXTURE AND *EXPRESSIVE* CAPABILITIES. BUT HE ALSO UNDERSTOOD IT'S *POWER*...

...AND IT'S POTENTIAL TO BE *EXPLOITED*.

* *'WORK WILL MAKE YOU FREE'*

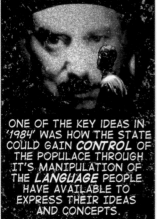

ONE OF THE KEY IDEAS IN '1984' WAS HOW THE STATE COULD GAIN **CONTROL** OF THE POPULACE THROUGH IT'S MANIPULATION OF THE **LANGUAGE** PEOPLE HAVE AVAILABLE TO EXPRESS THEIR IDEAS AND CONCEPTS.

ANOTHER MOTIVATION FOR HIS WRITING ORWELL DESCRIBES AS AN '**HISTORICAL IMPULSE**'. HE CONSIDERED IT IMPORTANT TO SEEK OUT THE **TRUTH** AND PRESERVE IT FOR POSTERITY...

HE WAS ALL TOO AWARE OF **HISTORIC FALSIFICATION**; HOW HISTORY IS ALWAYS "WRITTEN BY THE WINNERS" IN WAYS THAT **JUSTIFY** THE PRESENT AND THE **FUTURE**. THUS HISTORIC UNTRUTHS ARE USED AS **MORAL** JUSTIFICATION FOR **IMMORAL** ACTS.

LASTLY ORWELL CITES '**POLITICAL PURPOSE**' AS A DRIVE, USING THE WORD BROADLY. ORWELL'S FRIEND AND BIOGRAPHER **GEORGE WOODCOCK** WROTE:

"HE WAS MAINLY CONCERNED WITH THE IMPLEMENTIATION OF THOSE FAIRLY GENERAL IDEAS WHICH HE BROUGHT TOGETHER UNDER THE HEADING OF '**DECENCY**'...

...IDEAS LIKE BROTHERHOOD, FAIR PLAY AND HONEST DEALING.

ABOVE **ALL** HE THOUGHT IT IMPORTANT TO CREATE A WORLD IN WHICH EVERY MAN'S RIGHT TO **SELF-RESPECT** WOULD BE **JEALOUSLY PRESERVED**.

ORWELL SAID OF HIS MOTIVES FOR WRITING... "IT CAN BE SEEN HOW THESE VARIOUS IMPULSES MUST **WAR** AGAINST ONE ANOTHER..."

...I CANNOT SAY WITH CERTAINTY WHICH OF MY MOTIVES ARE THE **STRONGEST**, BUT I KNOW WHICH OF THEM DESERVE TO BE **FOLLOWED**.

IN 1935, BEFORE ORWELL FOUGHT IN SPAIN AND 13 YEARS BEFORE HE WROTE '1984', HE WROTE IN A POEM OF HIS STRUGGLE TO FIND A SUITABLE **POLITICAL IDENTITY** FOR HIMSELF. THE FINAL STANZA READ:

I dreamt I dwelt in marble halls...

...and woke to find it true. I wasn't born for an age like this...

Was Smith? Was Jones? Were YOU?

The man may also have been known as Omar Shamsoon.

He is thought to have once visited a mosque.

Christ! I can't believe this crap! The news has just become a government and media propaganda campaign. The 'War on Terror' so they have less resistance to the new laws they want to pass.

We're suppose to believe anything bad that happens is somehow connected to Muslims, so no one will question interventions in the Middle East.

They really want us to believe the war was for our safety. Like we're too dumb to see it was clearly about oil and a convenient distraction from domestic issues.

They just want us in a constant state of fear so we're easier to control. If you believe the news the world is full of nothing but terrorists and paedophiles.

Lucky the intellectuals amongst society aren't going to get sucked in by this bull shit.

46 26 56
BUS STOP

What if... just what if he's a terrorist... or a paedophile... or a terrorist paedophile!

107.

When dealing with propaganda in the modern world, it takes a lot to beat Rupert Murdoch, (and his well groomed son and heir Jimmy) as the world's largest and most right wing media baron. Having staunchly supported Reagan, Thatcher, Bush (Senior & Junior), Blair, & now, David Cameron, Murdoch makes sure he has a close relationship with those he backs; the classic case of 'you scratch my back, I'll scratch yours'. At this moment Murdoch and his sonny boy are looking to continue expanding the empire and to have more influence over British affairs.

Many fear that Britain is approaching a moment where Rupert Murdoch could win his bid for total control of BSkyB (from his already highly influential 40% share) and become Britain's answer to Berlusconi. He would then control half the television and newspaper market, and this would likely result in the decline of British TV, destroying fair competition, and we'll be likely to see the rise of Fox News style misinformation, that will make his current British right-wing clap-trap seem tame.

Murdoch enjoys a good war. From the Falklands, to Afghanistan and Iraq, he's made sure that his media has done more than it's fair share of warmongering and getting the public to back bloodshed. In the build up to the war on Iraq, no editor of a Murdoch-owned paper was allowed to oppose it. That's 175 editors worldwide and 40 million papers a week.
On 25 September 2002, The Sun helped to sell the Blair government's biggest lie, with a front-page headline declaring that Brits were "45 MINS FROM DOOM!" from WMDs. Other stories warned that we could be innundated with Anthrax or be under terrorist attack at any moment. Obviously, the solution to all this fear, potential death and outrage was to invade a country and take their oil. After all, The Sun's editorial made it clear that they shared Blair's "high moral values". Later, in a quote for the Sydney Telegraph, Murdoch stated: 'The greatest thing to come out of this for the world economy...would be $20 a barrel for oil.'...Yep Murdoch shared Blair's moral values alright.

He's even stooped as low as having political commentary by The Sun's Page 3 Girls (if we believe that the comments are actually made by the models). Entitled; "News In Briefs", the "*intelligent, vibrant young women*" have come out with all kinds of Orwellian praise for our brave moral leaders who took us to war, and encouraged us to boo-hiss the enemy, who needed to be crushed for the greater good. My favourite News In Briefs comment occurred when there was much discussion going on about whether the Iraq dossier was 'sexed up', if Saddam posed any threat of WMDs, and if the entire Iraq war was illegal. Fortunately, Page 3 "stunner" Zoe, 22 of London was there to put us straight; *'Zoe is certain that Blair was right to take Britain into the war with Iraq. She Said: "You don't need to be an international diplomat to realise the world is better off without Saddam. We should be proud of what has been achieved."'*

On January 26th 2007 at a conference in Switzerland, Murdoch was asked if News Corp had managed to shape the agenda on the war in Iraq. His answer surprised many when he openly admitted; "We tried...We basically supported the Bush policy in the Middle East...but we have been very critical of his execution." It's hard to see evidence of this criticism though. When the images of torture in Abu Ghraib were front page news, The Sun buried it on page 6, with less than a 1/4 page, 130 words and a very small picture. The next day, headlining with George W. Bush's version of events, they used 229 words, and presented a pro-Bush piece.

The Murdoch press is also notorious for stirring up hatred towards refugees and asylum seekers. When Rebekah Wade, took over as 'The Sun's' editor in 2003, she promptly launched a campaign against asylum seekers. A petition calling on Blair to 'stop Britain becoming a soft touch for illegal asylum seekers' is claimed to have attracted 600,000 signatories. In July 2003 The Sun went with the frontpage: 'Swan Bake - Asylum seekers steal the Queen's birds for barbecues'. The article claimed that: 'Callous asylum seekers are barbecuing the Queen's swans, the Sun can reveal'. In just 24 hrs, however, the Sun 'exclusive' was exposed as lies. Other BNP style propaganda included warnings against the 'asylum tide' and the need to 'stem the flood'; 'The laws aren't tough enough... the problem of asylum-seekers is out of control'. More skewed hysteria to cause prejudice and ignorance.

The most hysterical of Murdoch's mouthpieces however, is the rediculous so-called "fair and balanced" Fox News Channel. The most well known , bizarre and bigotted of the network's 'news commentators' are Bill O Reilley & Glenn Beck (featured on the next page), who are known for bullying guests, distorting truth and insighting hatred whilst claiming to be 'patriotic'. One of their latest accomplishments was the bogus "Ground-Zero" mosque story, where the network implied that the proposed community centre was an islamic plan to gloat at their enemies and perhaps even train terrorists. The fall-out from this story involved several hate attacks on muslims in the US, including the stabbing of a New York taxi driver. Well done Mr Murdoch, you must be very proud.

I LINE THEM UP SOMETIMES, IN THE GARDEN WHEN THE SUN IS HIGH... AND I GAZE FOR HOURS UPON THEM, SOFTLY SOBBING WITH WHAT I IMAGINE MIGHT BE JOY...

IS THERE A FINER SIGHT KNOWN TO MAN THAN A ROW OF SHOVELS GLISTENING LIKE DIAMONDS IN THE AFTERNOON SUNSHINE..?

YES, YES, THE SHOVELS ARE SUPERB.

NEIGHBOURS, EH? YOU KNOW, YOU COULD ALWAYS GO OVER THERE AND POUND THE FELLOW ON THE HEAD WITH A FIST...

THAT FIST COULD PERHAPS CONTAIN A SHOVEL?

IT REALLY ISN'T MY PLACE TO SAY...

DAMN IT! MISFIRE!

THERE'S A CLOSE CALL, EH? YOU KNOW WHAT TO DO, MY SNOTFACED LOINFRUITS...

OW!

GEDDIM!

113.

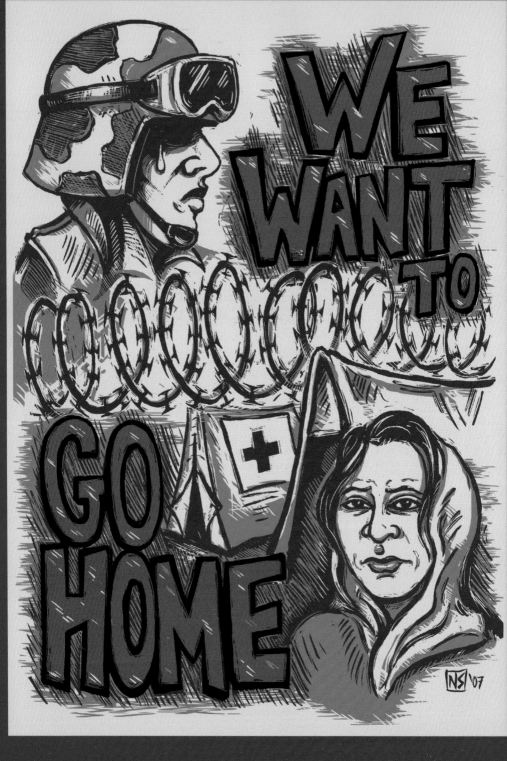

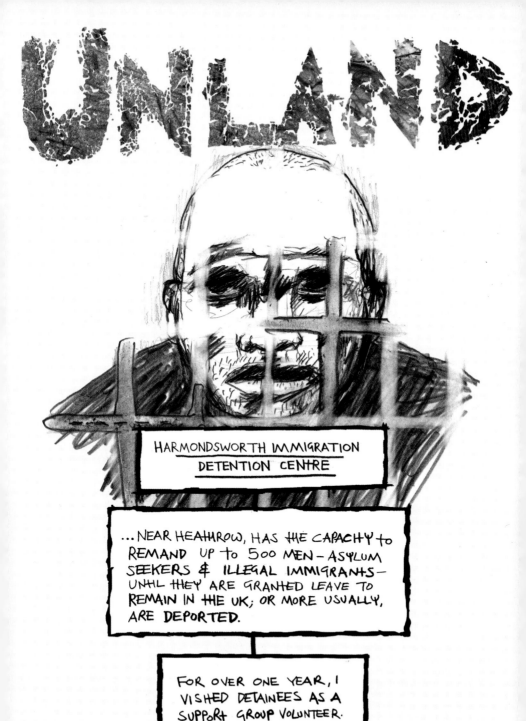

UNLAND

HARMONDSWORTH IMMIGRATION
DETENTION CENTRE

...NEAR HEATHROW, HAS THE CAPACITY TO
REMAND UP TO 500 MEN - ASYLUM
SEEKERS & ILLEGAL IMMIGRANTS -
UNTIL THEY ARE GRANTED LEAVE TO
REMAIN IN THE UK; OR MORE USUALLY,
ARE DEPORTED.

FOR OVER ONE YEAR, I
VISITED DETAINEES AS A
SUPPORT GROUP VOLUNTEER.

© CHRISTOPHER RAINBOW 2009 - WWW.ZIKOTOWN.COM

117.

LIFE AT HARMONDSWORTH IS HEAVILY REGULATED.

BLUE CHAIRS FOR VISITORS

RED CHAIRS FOR DETAINEES

VISITORS MUST GO THROUGH A PASSPORT CHECK, BODY SEARCH, METAL DETECTOR & MUST LEAVE ALL BAGS & PERSONAL ITEMS IN LOCKERS.

FOR MANY DETAINEES, THE SUDDEN TRANSITION FROM THE SEARCH FOR SANCTUARY TO DETAINMENT IS HARD TO COMPREHEND.

AS VISITORS, WE COULD OFFER ONLY A PATIENT & SYMPATHETIC EAR. SOME DETAINEES RESENTED THIS, ASSUMING THAT WE HAD THE POWER TO OBTAIN THEIR FREEDOM. MOST OFTEN, THE MEN I VISITED WERE SCARED, LONELY & GRATEFUL FOR COMPANY. THEY WOULD TELL OF HOW THEY WERE PLUCKED FROM LIVES IN THE UK; OR THEY WERE 'FAST-TRACKED' DIRECTLY FROM ENTRY INTO DETENTION.

THE ASYLUM SYSTEM IS WEIGHTED AGAINST THESE PEOPLE AT EVERY TURN. A WEB OF BUREAUCRACY ENSURES THAT MOST APPLICATIONS ARE AUTOMATICALLY DENIED, SO THAT FOR MANY, THEIR APPEAL AT HARMONDSWORTH'S IN-HOUSE COURT -ROOM REPRESENTS THEIR ONLY HEARING.

LEGAL SHARKS COMMONLY EXPLOIT DETAINEES - ARRIVING TO 'SIGN THEM UP', THEN DISAPPEARING, OFTEN FAILING TO EVEN ATTEND THEIR 'CLIENTS' HEARING.

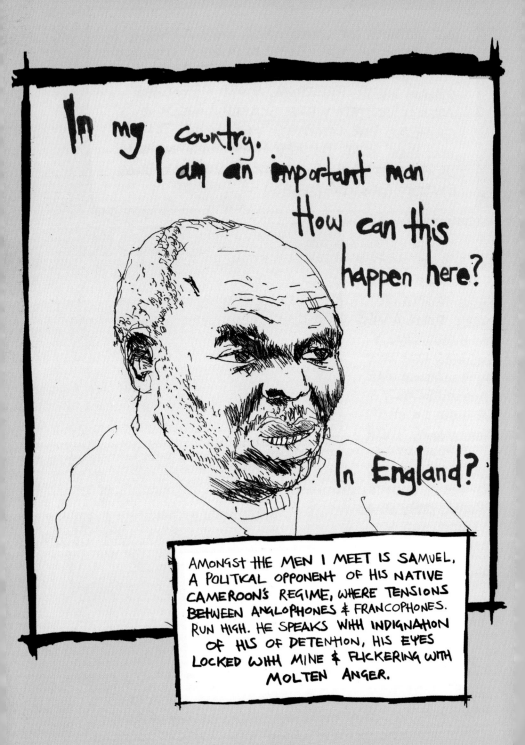

In my country,
I am an important man
How can this happen here?

In England?

AMONGST THE MEN I MEET IS SAMUEL,
A POLITICAL OPPONENT OF HIS NATIVE
CAMEROON'S REGIME, WHERE TENSIONS
BETWEEN ANGLOPHONES & FRANCOPHONES.
RUN HIGH. HE SPEAKS WITH INDIGNATION
OF HIS OF DETENTION, HIS EYES
LOCKED WITH MINE & FLICKERING WITH
MOLTEN ANGER.

WHEN I FLED CAMEROON, MY SISTERS WENT TO LIBERIA. NOW I CANNOT CONTACT THEM & THEY CANNOT CONTACT ME. I AM VERY WORRIED ABOUT THEM WITH THE WAR IN LIBERIA.

10 AM | I GET UP. I DON'T BOTHER WITH THE BREAKFAST. COLD SAUSAGES, COLD TOAST. A LOT OF DETAINEES MISS BREAKFAST.

10:30 – 11 AM | I WATCH TV

11–12 | I GO TO THE COMPUTER ROOM TO LISTEN TO CDS. I HAVE TO BE THERE AT 11 EXACTLY OR THEY DON'T LET ME IN.

12–1 | IS LUNCH. ALWAYS THE SAME. RICE.

1–4 | I LIE ON MY BED, SIESTA, EXCEPT I DON'T SLEEP.

4–5 | I CROSS BACK OVER TO THE COMPUTERS TO LISTEN TO CDS

5–6 | DINNER. RICE AGAIN. WITH CHICKEN OR BEEF.

6–7 | WATCH TV/LIE ON MY BED

7 | I TAKE MY MEDICATION.

AFTER 7 | I LIE ON MY BED UNTIL I FALL ASLEEP.

I WILL NEVER EVER

SINCE I AM HERE I DREAM OF GHOSTS

EVERYDAY IS THE SAME,

EVER GO BACK TO CAMEROON

THEY ~~GIVE~~ GIVE ME PILLS – NOW I FEEL NOTHING – JUST TIRED. STILL, IT IS BETTER THAN JAIL IN CAMEROON.

JOSEPH, ALSO CAMEROONIAN, WAS A TEACHER AND ACTIVIST. FOLLOWING VIOLENT ELECTIONS, HE FLED. HIS MOTHER, WHO STAYED, WAS KILLED.

121.

THE NEXT TIME I VISIT, DANIEL IS WEARING AN ILL-FITTING SUIT

HE APPEARS TIRED, GAUNT... DISTANT.

EARLIER, THAT MORNING, IMMIGRATION HAD ARRIVED TO DEPORT HIM.

HIS SKIN IS CUT & BRUISED.

AS I APPROACH, I SEE THAT HE IS SHAKING. HIS VOICE TREMBLES, BARELY AUDIBLE, AVOIDING EYE CONTACT.

"ALWAYS THREE COME" HE SAID, "AND EARLY, THIS TIME FOR ME"

ONCE ON THE PLANE, HELD FIRMLY BY TWO GUARDS, DANIEL BEGAN TO STRUGGLE. & SCREAM.

IT WORKED. BUT DANIEL HAD PAID WITH A BEATING.

THIS IS ONE TACTIC AVAILABLE TO THE DETAINEES, AS A PILOT HAS ABSOLUTE AUTHORITY TO REFUSE A PASSENGER.

AS HE REACHES FORWARD, I SEE HIS WRISTS ARE RAW & GASHED...

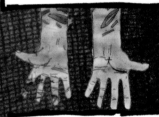

...THE HANDCUFF'S TRACE.

OTHER DETAINEES HAD WARNED OF SUCH OCCURENCES

I saw a guy from Sierra Leone. His face was red with blood. He had resisted deportation. I thought, 'next week, that could be me'.

It is not right that they can treat us like that. We are asylum seekers, but we are not animals.

I NEVER SAW DANIEL AGAIN.

ALTHOUGH SOME MONTHS LATER I RECEIVED AN EMAIL.

Hi,
This is Daniel, i just to say hi and thank u for the little help u rendered to me while in harmonsworthe i am really greatful, i pray God will help u in every of ur endervour. i hope u are coping fine, the guys have suceeded in bring me back to Nigeria but am still hiding from my persecutors, am in port harcourt south-east of Nigeria.
Thanks and God bless u.
Bye 4 now,
Daniel

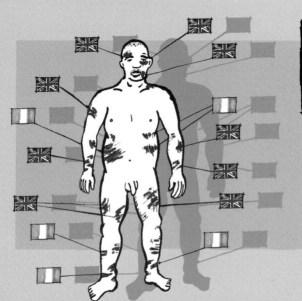

I OFTEN WONDER WHAT HAPPENED TO DANIEL, WHERE HE IS NOW — ALTHOUGH I PREFER NOT TO DWELL TOO LONG.

ALL I KNOW IS THAT HE WAS RETURNED TO NIGERIA — BUT NOT BEFORE MY COUNTRY, WHERE HE SOUGHT REFUGE, HAD INFLICTED SCARS OF ITS OWN.

WAR CANARY

BY SELINA LOCK & I. N. J. CULBARD

4TH AUGUST 1914: ENGLAND DECLARED WAR ON GERMANY, BUT I WAS BLISSFULLY UNAWARE. THE MASTER AND MISTRESS DIDN'T TELL ME ANYTHING.

GEORGE, THE FARMHAND, TRIED TO TELL ME.

I WENT INTO THE VILLAGE YESTERDAY, AND THEY SAY WE'RE AT WAR, WITH THE GERMANS.

ISN'T IT EXCITING?

DON'T BE SILLY, WE CAN'T BE AT WAR.

BOOM

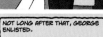

NOT LONG AFTER THAT, GEORGE ENLISTED.

I DECIDED THAT I WANTED TO DO MY BIT FOR THE WAR EFFORT TOO.

LABOUR EXCHANGE

TOWN HALL

IT WAS STRANGE, BUT EVER SO EXCITING, TO BE A MUNITIONS WORKER.

I SUPPOSE THE SHELLS I MADE KILLED HUNDREDS OF MEN, BUT WE DIDN'T THINK LIKE THAT AT THE TIME.

MUNITIONS WORK HAD ITS UPS ...

I COULD NEVER HAVE AFFORDED CLOTHES LIKE THESE IF I'D STAYED ON THE FARM.

AND ITS DOWNS ...

HEY, LOOK AT THE DIRTY CANARIES

MOST OF US HAD YELLOW FACES AND HANDS FROM WORKING WITH TNT.

SOME HAD FAR WORSE REACTIONS.

BUT ALL THAT MATTERED WAS THAT ...

THESE WOMEN ARE DOING THEIR BIT

LEARNING TO MAKE MUNITIONS

2008: TEN YEARS ON – A TALE OF TWO FACES

ONE FACE FOR PEACE...

WE'RE BACKING DOWN SOON, WE'RE OBLIGED TO DISARM...

IF YOU CANT BEAT 'EM, JOIN 'EM!!!

NEW LABOUR HAS TALKED ABOUT MULTILATERAL DISARMAMENT AND LIMITING IT'S NUCLEAR WEAPONS, BUT HAS GIVEN NO REAL ASSURANCES AT THE RECENT NNT (NON-PROLIFERATION TREATY) TALKS IN GENEVA.

ONE FACE FOR WAR

WE TRIDENTS ARE NO SPRING CHICKENS, WE'LL NEED TO BE REPLACED FOR THE GOOD OF THE COUNTRY.

...& WE'VE ALSO GOT TO SUPPORT OUR AMERICAN BROTHERS TOO, IN PLANNING THE CREATION OF MORE NATO MISSILE BASES IN CENTRAL EUROPE...

IF YOU CAN'T BEAT 'EM JOIN 'EM!!!

MORE WORRYINGLY, BRITAIN IS STILL TALKING ABOUT REPLACING IT'S TRIDENT MISSILES AND ALSO IS SUPPORTING THE US MISSILE DEFENSE SYSTEM, WHICH AS WELL AS USING BRITISH RAF RADAR BASES, INCLUDES THE PLANNED CREATION OF A NUCLEAR MISSILE BASE IN POLAND AND RADAR BASE IN THE CZECH REPUBLIC. SOME SAY THESE PLANS COULD CREATE ANOTHER ARMS RACE AND POSSIBLE COLD WAR, INCREASING WORLD TENSIONS. NATO ARE ALSO SUPPORTING THESE PLANS.

FOR MORE INFO GO TO: WWW.CNDUK.ORG

by paul stapleton

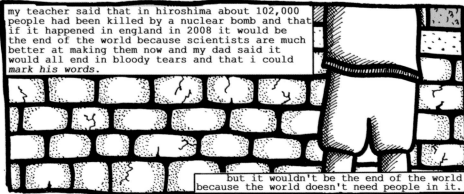

my teacher said that in hiroshima about 102,000 people had been killed by a nuclear bomb and that if it happened in england in 2008 it would be the end of the world because scientists are much better at making them now and my dad said it would all end in bloody tears and that i could *mark his words.*

but it wouldn't be the end of the world because the world doesn't need people in it.

because it wasn't hometime for about 24 minutes (because i didn't know the time exactly) i waited for my dad to take me home.

i counted 1800 seconds which meant he was late and i would have to get home myself.

i wasn't supposed to walk home on my own because of the *kids be aware* rule.

but i deduced that any strangers would be dead now and that it would be safe to walk home.

this is called *being rational*.

outside my school there were eight people who were dead.

and there were two people who were alive and they were screaming "*ohmygod ohmygodohfuckinggod*" like that so there were no spaces between each word.

because the nuclear bomb had caused *massive structural damage* everything looked different and it made me forget where i live.

to help me concentrate i made a faceshield so i could only see the sea which looked nearly the same as it did before the nuclear bomb.

i didn't have any cardboard so i used my hand.

then it was like it wasn't there.

but then i decided i needed to *keep my wits about me* so i put my faceshield away again.

my faceshield was only useful when i knew what i wanted to hide would go away.

like the children from the school opposite my school.

and the dog belonging to mrs. nation that always barks at me at weekends.

a woman was screaming "what have they done?" again and again.

i said "they have dropped a nuclear bomb"

i felt safe *being helpful* because there was a policeman with her.

Sainsbu

and i saw traffic wardens with guns and i thought it looked like a film all about war.

this is called *being helpful.*

then i started feeling sick.

a man said "where is your gasmask" and i ignored him because he was a stranger and i couldn't see his face.

then i saw i was only two streets away from my house.

then he said "you can't stay there you little idiot they're bringing the lorries out move."

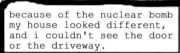

because of the nuclear bomb my house looked different, and i couldn't see the door or the driveway.

then i saw some of my hair fall out and there was some blood on my mouth.

then i heard a gun fire four times and some shouting.

then i was sick.

134.

when i'm feeling poorly i'm allowed to sleep on the couch and watch cartoons till i fall asleep.

but because of *massive damage to communications* the television and DVD player won't work.

i feel too sick and cold to do counting and i don't want to close my eyes because everything spins.

by paul stapleton   beat_bedsit@yahoo.co.uk   www.pogscribbles.org

Mazen Kerbaj: Diary In A Warzone.

The next 6 pages are a selection from Lebanese artist Mazen Kerbaj's Art Diary.

These pieces began in July 2006 when Lebanon was being bombed by the Israeli Air Force. Mazen's home city of Beiruit came under attack and he started to document what was going on around him by using his art and writing and putting it out there on his blog.

As the days passed, the bombing continued, and word got to Mazen about atrocities occurring elsewhere in the country, he continued to comment on what was happening.

These cartoons and artworks convey a wide range of raw emotions, switching quickly from wit and black humour, to anger, sadness and tragedy.

Mazen continues to post his artwork on his blog, and has many other drawings and comics to check out.

Visit:
http://mazenkerblog.blogspot.com/

it's small.
it has a white
ribbon.
there's plenty
of it in the
south.
and it
explodes
when you
play with
it.

they
left
us some
GiFTS

for you
and me
it looks like
a hand
grenade
with a stupid
white ribbon.
for a kid it
is a KINDER SURPRISE™

MAZEN '06

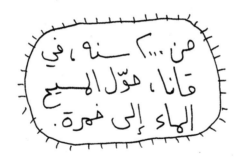

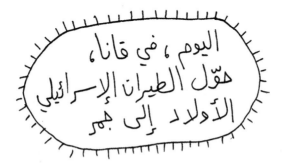

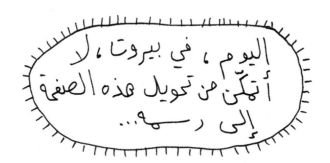

Translation:
2000 years ago, in Qana, jesus transformed water into wine.
Today, in Qana, the israeli air force transformed kids into ashes.
Today, in beirut, i am not able to transform this page into a drawing.

141.

Faith-Based TERRORISM

"LET'S CALL IT WHAT IT REALLY IS"

TEXT AND ART BY SPAIN

© SPAIN RODRIGUEZ '01

THE EVENTS OF SEPTEMBER ELEVENTH WERE HORRIFYING BUT NOT SURPRISING.

WHEN ASKED ABOUT MOSLEMS KILLED IN THE WORLD TRADE CENTER OSAMA BIN LADEN RESPONDED...

I HAVE READ THE HOLY QUIR'AN AND IT IS PERMITTED.

I WONDER IF THE FAMILY'S OF MOSLEM VICTIMS RECIEVED ANY SOLACE FROM HIS INTERPRETATION OF ISLAM'S HOLY BOOK?

BUT AMERICA IS NO STRANGER TO FAITH BASED TERRORISM. THE MURDEROUS "PRO-LIFE" MOVEMENT HAS A FEW BLOODY NOTCHES ON ITS BELT.

AND OF COURSE, AMERICA'S WOULD BE AYATOLAH, THE REVEREND JERRY FALWELL WAS RIGHT THERE TO WAG HIS FINGER IN OUR FACE.

...THE PAGANS, THE ABORTIONISTS, THE ATHEISTS, THE FEMINISTS. THE TELETUBBIES SET THE TONE FOR ALL THIS TO HAPPEN

IN THE MIDDLE AGES YOU COULD BUY "INDULGENCES" FROM THE CATHOLIC CHURCH THAT WOULD ABSOLVE YOU FROM ANY SIN, PAST OR FUTURE, YOU MIGHT COMMIT.

EVEN BACK THEN, PEOPLE COULD SEE THIS FOR THE TRANSPARENT FRAUD THAT IT WAS. THOSE WHO SPOKE OUT WERE LABELED HERETICS AND BURNT AT THE STAKE.

ADDICTED TO WAR

The War Profiteers

In the front lines of the **pro-war crowd** you'll find an assortment of **politicians**, **generals**, and **corporate executives**. If you ask them why they are so eager to go to war they'll give you **noble** and **selfless** reasons.

But what **really motivates** them to go to war are **somewhat less lofty** aims:

(146)

an illustrated exposé
by Joel Andreas

Who are the war profiteers?

Let's take a look at some of the men in Washington who are most **gung ho** about war...

Dick Cheney

Few politicians can match Dick Cheney's **enthusiasm for war** - or his record of **wanton destruction**. As George H.W. Bush's Secretary of Defense he presided over wars against Panama and Iraq, and then as Vice President under George W. Bush, he led the war drives against Afghanistan and Iraq.

Between wars, Dick has turned his attention from **destruction** to **construction** - that is post-war reconstruction. In 1995, he was named CEO of **Halliburton**, the world's largest oil services company and a major military contractor. After the first Gulf War, Halliburton was hired to help rebuild the Kuwaiti oil industry. Then after the second Gulf War, the company was back to **clean up the mess again** - for a **healthy fee.***

Halliburton

You've gotta hand it to Dick. He's got an **innovative business strategy** - first bomb it, then clean it up, then bomb it again, then clean it up again!

Halliburton is raking in hundreds of millions of dollars for feeding and housing U.S. troops in Iraq and it got the biggest post-war reconstruction prize - a **secret no-bid contract** to rebuild Iraqi oil facilities that will likely be worth billions.**

It's **nice** to have friends in Washington!

As Halliburton's CEO, Cheney was **rewarded handsomely,** pocketing millions in salary and stock options every year. He ended up as Halliburton's largest individual stockholder, with a $45 million stake.***

I **earned** every penny of it!

Cheney got **draft deferments** five times to avoid fighting in Vietnam. But he's eager to send **others** to **fight and die**, and then **reap the benefits**. He's served on the boards of several huge war contractors, and his wife - Lynne - joined the board of Lockheed Martin. After Cheney returned to the White House in 2001, Lockheed got the **biggest plum** in Pentagon history - a contract worth hundreds of billions to make the next generation of fighter jets. ****

We're just doing our **patriotic duty!**

148

"The Candidate from Brown & Root", -Robert Bryce, The Austin Chronicle, Aug. 25th, 2000

* "Contract Sport: What did the Vice-President do for Halliburton?" - Jane Mayer, New Yorker, Feb 16th & 23rd 2004

* * From Mayer's article; 'In 2000, Cheney left Halliburton to run for vice-president, but he retained $18 million in stock options and receives about $150,000 a year in deferred compensation.' The Halliburton contracts in Iraq 'earned' Cheney an estimated $5 million in stock whilst he was in office. This was a clear conflict of interest

* * * "Cheney's Five Draft Deferments", Katherine Seeyle, New York Times, May 1st 2004, & "Hard to Muzzle: The Retu... Of Lynne Cheney" -Jon Weiner, The Nation, Oct 2, 2000

As head of the Pentagon's Defense Policy Board, Richard Perle was a **chief architect** of both the **war on Iraq** and Donald Rumsfeld's efforts to "revolutionize" military technology. In 2001, Perle joined Henry Kissinger and other **Washington insiders** to form a company called Trireme Partners. Trireme raises **venture capital** from wealthy individuals and invests it in weapons companies, betting on those it expects will get lucrative government contracts.*

Richard Perle

Insider trading? We prefer to call it **guaranteed speculation!**

Henry

Perle has also served as an advisor to the **Israeli government.** Whether in Washington or Jerusalem, his advice is always the same...

War is **the answer!**

Perle has particularly pushed for war against three countries he considers Israel's main enemies – **Iraq, Iran** and **Syria.** **

One down, **two to go!**

Cheney, Perle and their friends go back and forth through a **revolving door** that connects jobs at the Pentagon, the White House, Congress and corporate military contractors. Lots of **money changes hands** in Washington as weapons manufacturers make **generous contributions** to politicians and politicians hand out **fat Pentagon contracts** to weapons manufacturers. This leads to all kinds of **shady agreements** and **overpriced goods.** ***

Here's to the Pentagon – the only place you can sell a 13¢ bol for $2,043!

The "War on Terrorism" has led to a tremendous **windfall** for the military contractors. The Army, Navy, and Air Force (and the contractors they represent) are lining up to get money for **expensive new weapons systems,** now packaged as indispensable for fighting terrorism.

We **can't afford** to be without it!

It's **vital** for **homeland defense!**

We have to close the **window of vulnerability!**

149

Seymour Hersh "Lunch with the Chairman: Why was Richard Perle meeting with Adnan Khashoggi?"
-New Yorker, March 17th, 2003

*Eg: A 1996 policy proposal, by Perle & other neo-conservative strategists for the Israeli govt entitled "A Clean Break: A New Strategy For Securing The Realm". The proposal can be found at:
www.israelieconomy.org/strat1.htm

**Arms, Politics & the Economy - Robert Higgs

In fact, under the banner of funding the "War on Terrorism," Congress has **abandoned** efforts to avoid budget deficits. Instead, every year it gives the Pentagon what amounts to a **blank check**.

For **whatever** it takes...

PAY TO THE ORDER OF **PENTAGON** $ _____

_____ DOLLARS

U.S. Congress

After the end of the **Cold War,** many in Washington were reconsidering the **humongous size** of the military budget, which had converted the U.S. from the world's biggest lender into the **world's biggest debtor.**

USA

Bonds, anyone? T-bills?

Ouch! That **hurts!**

USA

In an effort to balance the federal budget, politicians were beginning to **trim** the Pentagon's **toenails**.

After September 11 all this changed. Bush and the Congress started to pump up the Pentagon's **bloated budget** without restraint.

USA

Even Congressional opposition to the far-fetched **"missile defense program"** collapsed.

Beep Beep

Missile defense, like the "War on Terrorism," **promises to protect Americans** from danger while actually creating a much **more dangerous world.** If other countries think there is any chance the U.S. could block their missiles, they will feel **vulnerable** to U.S. attack. China has already promised to build more and better missiles which could overwhelm the U.S. "missile shield." This will spur a **nuclear arms race in Asia.**

If **China** builds more nuclear missiles, then **India** will. If India does, then **Pakistan** will. If Pakistan...

In 1972, the U.S. and the U.S.S.R. signed the **ABM Treaty** to try to avoid this kind of arms race. In order to pursue missile defense, the U.S. **unilaterally scrapped** the treaty. But that didn't bother missile defense proponents.*

Hey, the world's changed. **We can win an arms race** with anyone!

In this spirit, Congress **rejected the nuclear test ban treaty** (which has been signed by 164 countries) and it continues to finance nuclear weapons research and production. In fact, the Pentagon is eager to develop a new arsenal of small **"battlefield" nuclear weapons.** **

The U.S. is keeping enough nuclear firepower to **wipe out** most of **humanity.**

Just to be safe!

As potential nuclear targets in Russia have declined, the Pentagon has been retargeting its missiles at **"every reasonable adversary."**

Which makes other countries feel like they better **hurry up** and get nuclear weapons themselves ***

(151)

***The 1972 Anti-Ballistic Missile Treaty had outlawed defensive missile systems. See "Washington's New Freedom & New Worries in the Post-ABM-Treaty Era" -New York Times, Dec 15th, 2001
* * "Plan for New Nukes Clears Major Hurdle" - Los Angeles Times, May 10th, 2002... & for updates on U.S. nuclear weapons policies, see the Physicians for Social Responsibility website: www.psr.org
* * *"U.S. urged to Cut 50% of A-Arms: Soviet Breakup Is Said To Allow Radical Shift in Strategic Targeting, -Washington Post, Jan 6th, 1991

In the post-Cold War world order, the U.S. does not seem to want to be bound by any arms treaties. It **refuses to sign** a new protocol to the 1972 biological weapons treaty because it would require **international inspections** of its **biological weapons research facilities**, where it is creating **deadly new strains** including highly lethal **powdered anthrax.** U.S. officials say they are only creating germ weapons in order to study how to defend against them.*

Of course, we would **never** use them **ourselves!**

But can other countries **trust** a government that bombed Hiroshima and Nagasaki and actually developed plans to use **smallpox** and other biological weapons against **Vietnam** and **Cuba?**
**

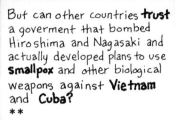

Would you?

And U.S. **"weaponized germs"** not only represent a threat to people in other countries.

What if some of the Pentagon's powdered anthrax got into the hands of **some fanatic here** in the United States?

During the Cold War, the Soviet Union was a serious military competitor for the United States. Today, the U.S. maintains a huge war machine despite the **lack of any serious competition.** The U.S. military budget is now larger than the next 25 biggest spenders **put together!** It makes up a full **36%** of **total global military spending.*****

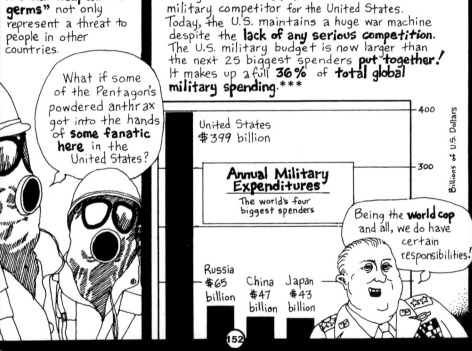

Annual Military Expenditures
The world's four biggest spenders

United States
$399 billion

Russia
$65 billion

China
$47 billion

Japan
$43 billion

400

300

Billions of U.S. Dollars

Being the **world cop** and all, we do have certain responsibilities!

152

* "U.S. Seeks Changes In Germ War Pact" - New York Times, Nov.1, 2001, & "U.S. Recently produced Anthrax in a Highly Lethal Powder Form" - New York Times, Dec. 13th, 2001
** Germs: Biological Weapons and America's Secret War - William Broad & Judith Miller 2001
*** Data is from following years: U.S, 2004; Japan, 2002; Russia and China, 2001. For updated info on world & U.S. Military spending go to www.cdi.org

The High Price of Militarism

Maintaining this huge military machine is **not cheap**. Every year the U.S. spends **hundreds of billions** of dollars on the military.*

This figure does not include tens of billions spent on the military occupations of Afghanistan and Iraq

$399,000,000,000
military budget
2004 fiscal year

$308 billion — 2001
$351 billion — 2002
$396 billion — 2003
$470 billion (proposed) — 2007

Since 1948 the U.S. has spent more than **$15 trillion** to build up its military might. Just **how much** is $15,000,000,000,000 **worth**? **

Lemme see...

My God!

It adds up to **more than** the cumulative monetary value of **all human-made wealth** in the U.S.!***

In other words, the government has spent more on the military over the last four decades than the value of **all the factories**, machinery, roads, **bridges**, water and sewage systems, **airports**, railroads, **power plants**, office buildings, shopping centers, **schools**, hospitals, hotels, **houses**, etc., in the U.S. **put together!**

Wow!

153

* **2001-2007 Center for Defense Information: www.cdi.org.uk/ New York Times**

** **Center for Defense Information: www.cdi.rog/issues/milspend.html**

*** **Michael Renner: National Security: The Economic & Environmental Dimensions (World Watch Institute)**

The Magick GUN

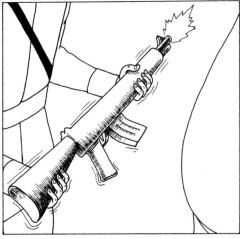

ALEISTHERRSCHULZE © 2007

159.

REMEMBER THE MAINE!

by Mack White

JANUARY 25, 1898– THE U.S.S. **MAINE** ARRIVES IN **CUBA** ...

CUBA AT THIS TIME IS IN THE EARLY STAGES OF A "WAR OF INDEPENDENCE" WITH **SPAIN**. SENSATIONAL REPORTS IN THE **AMERICAN** PRESS ABOUT **SPANISH** MISTREATMENT OF THE **CUBANS** HAVE CAUSED WIDESPREAD PUBLIC OUTRAGE AND CALLS FOR **AMERICAN INTERVENTION** ...

THERE IS A STORY THAT WHEN NEWSPAPER PUBLISHER **WILLIAM RANDOLPH HEARST** SENT NOTED ARTIST **FREDERIC REMINGTON** TO **CUBA** TO COVER THE STORY, **REMINGTON** FOUND THINGS QUIET AND CABLED **HEARST**: "THERE WILL BE NO WAR." **HEARST** REPLIED: "YOU FURNISH THE PICTURES. **I'LL** FURNISH THE WAR." **HEARST** ALWAYS DENIED THE STORY ...

BUT WHETHER THE STORY IS TRUE OR NOT, THERE IS NO DOUBT THAT THE **PRESS** MANIPULATED **PUBLIC OPINION** WITH WILDLY EXAGGERATED STORIES ...

SPANIARDS SEARCH WOMEN ON AMERICAN STEAMERS

FROM AN ILLUSTRATION BY REMINGTON

AS A RESULT OF THIS GROWING **ANTI-SPANISH** SENTIMENT, **PRESIDENT McKINLEY** SENDS THE **MAINE** TO **CUBA** TO MONITOR THE SITUATION. FOR THE NEXT FEW WEEKS, THE SHIP SITS PEACEFULLY IN **HAVANA HARBOR**. THEN, ON THE NIGHT OF FEBRUARY 15...

THE BLAST KILLED **266** MEN. THE PRESS IMMEDIATELY BLAMED IT ON A **SPANISH** MINE. A SUBSEQUENT INQUIRY DETERMINED IT TO BE DUE TO UNKNOWN **INTERNAL** CAUSES, BUT BY THAT TIME IT WAS TOO LATE— **AMERICA** HAD ALREADY GONE TO WAR UNDER THE BATTLE CRY "**REMEMBER THE MAINE!**" WHEN IT WAS ALL OVER, **SPAIN** CEDED CUBA AND SIX OTHER COLONIES TO **AMERICA** ...

INMEMORIAM

IT MAY BE TRITE TO COMPARE POLITICIANS TO HITLER, JUST BECAUSE ONE DOES NOT LIKE THEM. IN GEORGE W. BUSH'S CASE, IT IS SOMEWHAT LESS INAPPROPRIATE THAN IN OTHER'S — AND NOT ONLY BECAUSE OF HIS DESTRUCTIVE POLITICS. THERE'S ALSO THE...

BUSH·NAZI CONNECTION

©MARCEL RUIJTERS 2004

MUCH HAS BEEN SAID ABOUT HITLER'S AFFINITY FOR THE OCCULT (ALONG WITH SOME OF HIS CRONIES LIKE HESS OR HIMMLER).

WHILE HITLER'S CHARISMATIC SPELL OVER THE GERMAN CROWDS DURING HIS SPEECHES WAS UNCANNY AND CAN BE EASILY LABELLED AS DEMONIC, HIS METEORIC RISE TO POWER HAS LITTLE TO DO WITH HIS ASTRAL SIGN OR THE LEGENDARY SPEAR OF LONGINUS. BAH! HUMBUG!

LIKE ANY ASPIRING POLITICIAN, HITLER NEEDED MONEY, LOTS OF MONEY. AND CORPORATE BUSINESS WAS EAGER TO PROVIDE IT.

THE LIST OF NAZI SPONSORS IS FAIRLY WELL-KNOWN TODAY: I.G. FARBEN, KRUPP, BOSCH, SIEMENS, ITT, FORD, DUPONT, GENERAL ELECTRIC, STANDARD OIL, AND SO ON. WITHOUT A DOUBT, THE MOST GENEROUS SUPPORTER WAS FRITZ THYSSEN, THEN HEAD OF THE ALMIGHTY THYSSEN CORPORATION.

OF COURSE, MANY CORPORATIONS FINANCED THE NAZIS FOR OPPORTUNISTIC REASONS, BUT THYSSEN'S RELATIONSHIP WITH HITLER IS REPORTED AS A CORDIAL ONE.

THE N.S.D.A.P. WAS ABLE TO BUY THE PRESTIGIOUS "BRAUNE HAUS" IN MUNICH AND MAKE IT THEIR HEADQUARTERS, THANKS TO A GIFT OF 100.000 GOLD MARKS FROM THYSSEN IN 1923.

WE ARE TALKING OLD MONEY HERE, BUT IT WAS THE GREAT PATRIARCH AUGUST THYSSEN (1842-1926) WHO HAD MADE THE COMPANY INTO ONE OF GERMANY'S LEADING INDUSTRIES BY THE BEGINNING OF THE 20TH CENTURY. WITHOUT ITS GUNS AND CANNONS, GERMANY COULD NOT HAVE STARTED WORLD WAR I. A WAR THAT LEFT THE COUNTRY IN RUINS AND THE THYSSENS WITH EVEN GREATER RICHES. AUGUST DIVIDED THE CAPITAL BETWEEN HIS TWO SONS FRITZ AND HEINRICH. ONE HAD TO SIDE WITH THE NAZIS, THE OTHER TO OPPOSE THEM. AT LEAST, TO THE PUBLIC EYE...

SINCE THE MID 19TH CENTURY, THE THYSSENS HAD BEEN POWERFUL ENOUGH TO ESTABLISH THEIR OWN BANKS WITH RESPECTABLE-SOUNDING NAMES. FRITZ THYSSEN WOULD PROVE HIMSELF WORTHY OF CARRYING ON THIS FAMILY TRADITION AND WAS EVEN SKILLFUL ENOUGH TO HIDE THEIR ASSETS FROM THE ALLIED FORCES AFTER WW2!

BHS
ROTTERDAM
HOLLAND
HAMBURG
BERLIN
POLAND
SILESIA
RUHR REGION
FRANCE
GERMANY
SWITZERLAND
AUSTRIA

MUCH OF THEIR MONEY-LAUNDERING WENT THROUGH THE BANK VOOR HANDEL EN SCHEEPVAART (BANK FOR COMMERCE AND SHIPPING), CLEVERLY ESTABLISHED IN HOLLAND IN 1926.

IN HIS APOLOGETIC, GHOST-WRITTEN AUTOBIOGRAPHY "I PAID HITLER", THYSSEN CLAIMED THAT HE QUIT SUPPORTING THE NAZI PARTY IN 1939 AFTER HE REALISED WHAT THEY WERE PLANNING FOR THE JEWS. HE FURTHER CLAIMED THAT HIMSELF WAS PERSECUTED BY THE NAZI, FLED TO SWITZERLAND AND WAS FINALLY CAPTURED IN 1942 IN VICHY-FRANCE. HOWEVER, OFFICIAL DOCUMENTS PROVE THAT HE WAS ABLE TO TRAVEL FREELY UNTIL THEN.

ANYWAY, MUCH OF THE MONEY THAT WAS BEING MADE WENT TO AMERICA VIA THE BHS-OWNED UNION BANKING CORPORATION, LOCATED AT 39 BROADWAY.

IT'S HERE WHERE WE MEET PRESCOTT SHELDON BUSH.

BROADWAY

165.

PRESCOTT BUSH WAS MADE VICE-PRESIDENT OF THE U.B.C. BY HIS FATHER-IN-LAW, GEORGE HERBERT WALKER IN 1926 AFTER MARRYING WALKER'S DAUGHTER DOROTHY.
TOGETHER WITH HIS PARTNERS HARRIMAN AND BROWN BROTHERS, HE IS AT THIS POINT AN EMPLOYEE OF THE THYSSEN FIRM.
HE IS ALSO INVOLVED WITH THE NEWLY FORMED GERMAN STEEL TRUST, THANKS TO DILLON READ, A FRIEND OF HIS FATHER SAMUEL BUSH.

AH... ANOTHER GOOD DAY'S WORK!

MANY WALL STREET PLAYERS OF THE ERA WERE ENDORSING TOTALITARIANISM: THE BUSHES, WALKERS, HARRIMANS, LOVETTS, BROWN BROTHERS (WHO HAD BECOME RICH FROM SHIPPING SLAVE COTTON) THE ROCKEFELLERS, MONTAGU COLLET NORMAN OF THE BANK OF ENGLAND. EVEN THE WARBURGS, WHO STAYED IN GERMANY UNTIL 1938, WHEN LIFE HAD ALREADY BECOME UNBEARABLE FOR COMMON JEWS.

FASCISM = POLITICS X CORPORATE BUSINESS

IN 1927, AVERELL HARRIMAN REPORTED TO THE UBC ABOUT HIS FRUITFUL MEETING WITH MUSSOLINI.

HARRIMAN AND WALKER HAD TAKEN CONTROL OF THE STEAMSHIP COMPANY HAMBURG-AMERIKA LINE, BACK IN 1920. IN THE YEARS PRIOR TO HITLER'S ELECTION AS CHANCELOR IN 1933, THE FIRM HAD BEEN CRUCIAL FOR THE ARMAMENT OF THE S.S. AND S.A. TONS OF REVOLVERS AND MACHINE GUNS WERE SMUGGLED INTO THE COUNTRY VIA HOLLANDS RIVER DELTA TO OBSTRUCT AND TERRORISE THE OPPOSITION. THE GUNS WERE MADE IN THE UNITED STATES BY REMINGTON AND THOMSON.

MAX WARBURG OF HAMBURG, THEIR REPRESENTATIVE AT THE TIME, PROTECTED THE BUSH-WALKER CLAN FROM ALLEGATIONS OF SUPPORT TO ANTI-SEMITIC FORCES IN EUROPE. WITH THIS FAMOUS JEWISH BANKER AS THEIR ASSOCIATE, THEIR BUSINESS SEEMED ALL KOSHER TO THE AMERICAN SPONSORS.

WALKER, HARRIMAN AND BUSH WERE NOT TOO BOTHERED BY BEING PARTNERS TO TOP NAZI FRIEDRICH FLICK, EITHER, WHO, TOGETHER WITH THYSSEN, OWNED THE COAL AND ZINC MINES AND STEEL WORKS OF THE CONSOLIDATED SILESIAN STEEL CORPORATION, SITUATED IN SOUTHERN POLAND.

1934, PROBLEMS AROSE WITH POLISH ACCUSATIONS OF MISMANAGEMENT AND EMBEZZLEMENT. FLICK RETALIATED BY REPLACING THE POLISH WORKERS WITH GERMANS TO CONTINUE HIS CONTRIBUTION TO THE BUILD-UP OF HITLER'S WAR MACHINE. THE DISPUTE WAS ENDED BY THE BLITZKRIEG.

JETZT GEHT'S LOS!

FOR MOST PEOPLE, THE START OF THE SECOND WORLD WAR FELT PRETTY MUCH LIKE THE END OF THE WORLD, BUT NOT FOR THE WALKER-BUSH DYNASTY AND THEIR FRIENDS.

HARRIMAN INTERNATIONAL C°, LED BY AVERELL HARRIMAN'S COUSIN OLIVER, HAD BEEN RESPONSIBLE FOR GERMAN EXPORTS TO THE U.S. SINCE 1933, AS WAS AGREED BETWEEN HJALMAR SCHACHT AND JOHN FOSTER DULLES.

WHILE MILLIONS WERE SLAUGHTERED, BUSINESS WENT ON AS USUAL. THAT IS, UNTIL OCTOBER 20 1942. UNDER THE 'TRADING WITH THE ENEMY' ACT, THE GOVERNMENT SEIZED THE STOCK SHARES OF THE UNION BANKING CORP. (OF WHICH THE BULK WAS OWNED BY E. ROLAND HARRIMAN) ON THE 28TH OF OCTOBER. ALSO THE HOLLAND-AMERICAN TRADING CORP AND SEAMLESS STEEL EQUIPMENT CORP, RUN BY THE UBC, FOLLOWED. NOVEMBER 17, INTERESTS IN THE SILESIAN-AMERICAN CORP WERE SEIZED.
BUT THAT WAS ABOUT ALL THE ROOSEVELT ADMINISTRATION DID AGAINST THESE BLATANT ACTS OF TREACHERY. WAS IT BECAUSE THE SCANDAL WOULD BE TOO DEMORALIZING FOR THE TROOPS WHO HAD BEEN SENT INTO WAR A YEAR BEFORE?

NONE OF THESE TRAITORS WAS BROUGHT TO JUSTICE. THE ONLY 'VICTIM' WAS BUSH'S OIL PARTNER WILLIAM FARISH I, WHO DIED OF A HEART ATTACK AFTER THE HEARINGS.

WILL FARISH III, THE SOLE HEIR, IS STILL A FRIEND OF THE BUSH'S.

IN A MOVE TO CLEAR THE FAMILY'S NAME, GEORGE H.W. BUSH, WHO HAD TURNED 18, WAS SENT TO JOIN THE AIR FORCE. GEORGE BUSH WAS SHOT DOWN IN A BATTLE OVER THE PACIFIC AND GIVEN A MEDAL OF HONOR. HOWEVER, RUMOR HAS IT THAT HE BAILED OUT TOO SOON AND LEFT HIS TWO CO-PILOTS TO DIE IN THE PLANE, JUST TO SAVE HIS OWN HIDE.

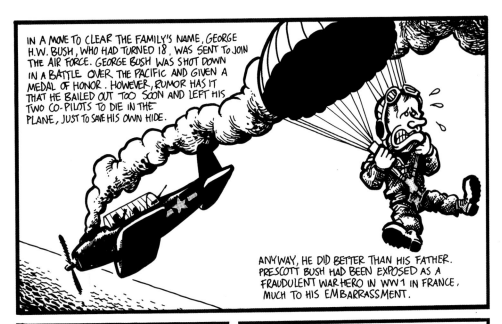

ANYWAY, HE DID BETTER THAN HIS FATHER. PRESCOTT BUSH HAD BEEN EXPOSED AS A FRAUDULENT WAR HERO IN WW1 IN FRANCE, MUCH TO HIS EMBARRASSMENT.

1945. HITLER COMMITTED SUICIDE. THE NIGHTMARE OF W.W.2 WAS FINALLY OVER. OR WAS IT?

THEN THERE WAS, AMONG OTHER THINGS, THE MATTER OF THE NAZI LOOT, WHICH WAS BEING RAPIDLY RELOCATED OVER THE GLOBE.

CONSIDERING THE FACT THAT SUCH POWERFUL AMERICANS HAD BEEN IN LEAGUE WITH THE NAZIS, IT COMES AS NO SURPRISE THAT SO MANY GOT AWAY. FOR INSTANCE, FRIEDRICH FLICK ONLY SERVED THREE YEARS IN JAIL, THEN GOT HIS MONEY BACK AND DIED A BILLIONAIRE IN 1972. THE MAN WHO PARDONED FLICK IN 1951 WAS JOHN JAY MCCLOY, THE LEGAL COUNSELLOR FOR I.G. FARBEN IN THE U.S. THIS WAS THE FIRM THAT OPERATED THE CONCENTRATION CAMPS. MCCLOY WAS ONE OF THE MEN THAT OBSTRUCTED THE BOMBING OF THE RAILWAYS TO THOSE CAMPS. HE WENT ON TO WORK FOR THE FORD FOUNDATION (THE BIGGEST AMERICAN NAZI SPONSOR), THE MANHATTAN CHASE BANK AND EVENTUALLY BECAME PRESIDENT OF THE WORLD BANK. HE ALSO PARDONED THYSSEN, SCHACHT AND KRUPP.

JUST DON'T DO IT AGAIN!

tap

GENERAL WILLIAM H. DRAPER JR. WHO HAD BEEN WORKING WITH BUSH FOR THE THYSSENS AND FINANCED THE INTERNATIONAL EUGENETICS CONGRESS IN NEW YORK IN 1932, WAS APPOINTED TO "DE-NAZIFY" GERMAN CORPORATE BUSINESS.

ALSO ALLEN DULLES WORKED WITH BUSH AS A LEGAL COUNSELLOR (SPY) FOR I.G. FARBEN AND STANDARD OIL, WHICH WERE CONTROLLED BY THE ROCKEFELLERS BEFORE, DURING AND AFTER THE WAR.

TOGETHER WITH GERMAN MASTER-SPY GERHARD GEHLEN, DULLES ARRANGED THE SECRET IMMIGRATION OF 760 SCIENTISTS WHO WERE HARD-CORE NAZIS INTO THE U.S. THIS IS NOW KNOWN AS "PROJECT PAPERCLIP".

IN 1951, FRITZ THYSSEN DIED IN ARGENTINA. PRESCOTT BUSH AND HIS FATHER-IN-LAW RECLAIMED THE UNION BANK FROM THE U.S. ALIEN PROPERTY CUSTODIAN AND WERE ABLE TO CASH IN THEIR SHARES FOR A COOL $1.500.000 EACH.

ALL THAT TROUBLE FOR NOTHING! ACH!

IN SHORT, IT TOOK QUITE SOME CLEVER SCHEMING TO CONCEAL THE ORIGIN OF THE BUSH FORTUNE AND CHANGE THEIR PUBLIC IMAGE FROM THIS...

New York Herald Tribune

THYSSEN HAD 3 MILLION CASH IN MY VAULTS

OH SHIT!

...TO THIS: IN 1952, PRESCOTT BUSH WAS ELECTED AS SENATOR. AND HIS OFFSPRING? PRESIDENTIAL MATERIAL!

THANK YOU AND GOD BLESS AMERICA!

THE END

ROCKET SCIENCE

THE *NUCLEAR DESTRUCTION* OF *NAGASAKI* AND *HIROMISHA* AT THE END OF *WORLD WAR II*...

...HAD ESTABLISHED THE *REALITY* OF HUMANKIND BEING *CAPABLE* OF BUILDING AND *DEPLOYING* A *WEAPON* CAPABLE OF A LEVEL OF *DEVASTATION* PREVIOUSLY THOUGHT *IMPOSSIBLE*....

AND SO, IN A SITUATION OF *WAR*, WHERE A *SINGLE* WEAPON WAS CAPABLE OF DESTROYING AN *ENTIRE* CITY IN AN *INSTANT*...

...THE *KEY FACTOR* THUS BECAME THAT OF *SPEED* AND HOW *QUICKLY ONE* NATION COULD *DEPLOY* IT'S *WEAPONS* AGAINST *ANOTHER*.

IT WAS IN *THIS* RESPECT THAT THE DEVELOPMENT OF *ROCKET TECHNOLOGY* BECAME *CRUCIAL*.

AS *BERLIN* FELL, BOTH THE *RUSSIANS* AND THE *AMERICANS*, EACH IDEOLOGICALLY *OPPOSED* TO THE *NAZI'S* BUT IN ALL OTHER RESPECTS *RIVALS*, RACED TO *CLAIM* THE *TECHNOLOGY* THAT WOULD BE UP FOR GRABS, *ESPECIALLY* THE *ROCKET SCIENCE* THAT THE NAZIS HAD *DEVELOPED*.

'MITTELWERK'...

...AN UNDERGROUND *ROCKET FACTORY* BUILT IN A TUNNEL SYSTEM BENEATH THE *KIHNSTEIN MOUNTAIN*...

...AND WORKED BY CONCENTRATION CAMP *SLAVES*...

...PRODUCED *THOUSANDS* OF THE *V2* ROCKETS...

...THAT WERE LAUNCHED AGAINST *LONDON* AND OTHER EUROPEAN CITIES.

BUT STILL THE **DEATHS** OF WORKERS **OUTNUMBERED** THOSE KILLED IN THE **ACTUAL** V2 ROCKET **ATTACKS**.

ONE **SURVIVOR** DESCRIBED MITTELWERK AS **'THE ANTE-CHAMBERS OF HELL'**.

THE **REAL** TERROR OF THE **V2'S** WAS **PSYCHOLOGICAL** AND THE NAZIS **KNEW** IT.

BUT THE TECHNOLOGY THAT **PROPELLED** THEM WAS WHAT **STALIN** AND **ROOSEVELT** WERE INTERESTED IN. BOTH THE **RUSSIANS** AND THE **AMERICANS** WANTED TO CAPTURE **NAZI ROCKET SCIENCE** FOR THEMSELVES IN ORDER TO HELP THEM DEVELOP **INTERCONTINENTAL BALLISTIC MISSILES**.

AT THE **END** OF THE WAR THE **AMERICANS** CAPTURED **THREE HUNDRED** TRAIN-LOADS OF **V2'S** WHICH WERE THEN SENT BACK TO THE **UNITED STATES**.

173.

MORE *CRUCIALLY*, THE AMERICAN *'OPERATION PAPERCLIP'*
SUCCESSFULLY *SMUGGLED* OUT OF GERMANY *126* OF THE
V2'S *SCIENTISTS* AND *ENGINEERS*, WHOSE NUMBER
INCLUDED ROCKET PIONEER *WHERNER VON BRAUN.*

VON BRAUN, A ROCKET GENIUS, HAD BEEN APPOINTED
MITTELWERKS *DIRECTOR*, THOUGH, IN REALITY, HE WAS AS
POWERLESS AS THE *PRISONERS*:

IT WAS *HELLISH*...
I WAS TOLD BY THE
SS GUARDS THAT I SHOULD
'MIND MY OWN BUSINESS',
OR FIND *MYSELF* IN THE
SAME STRIPED
FATIGUES.

THOUGH BY RIGHTS MANY SHOULD HAVE BEEN
TRIED AS *WAR CRIMINALS*, NEARLY *500 NAZI SCIENTISTS*
ENTERED THE U.S *BYPASSING* OFFICIAL CHANNELS SO THAT
THEY COULD BE PUT TO WORK DEVELOPING U.S MISSILE AND
ROCKET TECHNOLOGY AT VARIOUS *MILITARY INSTALLATIONS.*

THE SOVIETS, MEANWHILE,
HAD ALSO CAPTURED V2
TECHNOLOGY. *20 MILLION*
RUSSIANS HAD *DIED*
DURING WORLD WAR II...

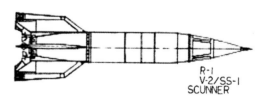

R-1
V-2/SS-1
SCUNNER

...SUCH A LOSS WOULD NEVER BE REPEATED.
USING STOLEN *NAZI SCIENCE* THEY BUILT
A *REPLICA* OF THE V-2 CALLED THE *R-1*,
THOUGH THE WEIGHT OF THE *NUCLEAR
WARHEADS* NECESSITATED THE DEVELOP-
MENT OF A MORE POWERFUL *BOOSTER.*

AND SO FOR THE NEXT *THREE DECADES*, BUILDING UPON THE ROCKET TECHNOLOGY STOLEN AS *SPOILS* OF *WAR*...

...BOTH THE *SOVIETS* AND THE *AMERICANS* EMBARKED ON PROGRAMS OF BUILDING INCREASINGLY DEVASTATING *INTERCONTINENTAL BALLISTIC MISSILES*.

WE DON'T PROPOSE TO SIT HERE IN OUR *ROCKING CHAIR* WITH OUR HANDS FOLDED AND LET THE *COMMUNISTS* SET UP ANY GOVERNMENT IN THE *WESTERN HEMISPHERE*.

LYNDON BAINES JOHNSON

WHETHER YOU *LIKE IT* OR *NOT*, *HISTORY* IS ON *OUR* SIDE. WE WILL *BURY* YOU.

NIKITA KHRUSHCHEV

THIS *'ARMS RACE'*, FUELLED BY SOVIET AND U.S *RIVALRY*...

...AND DRIVEN BY *ANXIETIES* ABOUT HOW *AGGRESSIVELY* EACH NATION WAS PREPARED TO PURSUE ITS *IDEOLOGIES*...

...BECAME KNOWN AS *'THE COLD WAR'*.

EXCERPT FROM *'SO LONG, MAJOR TOM'* BY PAUL O'CONNELL, *WWW.SOUNDOFDROWNING.COM*

175.

176.

MY FIRST POSTING WAS TO LEAVE FROM SOUTH-
-AMPTON IN THE SUMMER OF '41. DUE TO A
TRANSPORT PROBLEM IT SAILED WITHOUT ME.

THAT SHIP WAS SUNK.
EVERYBODY DIED.

SURVIVING A WAR HAS AS MUCH
TO DO WITH CHANCE AND LUCK
AS ANYTHING ELSE.

I SERVED ON-BOARD THE HMS ORWELL IN THE WINTER OF 1942.

WE WERE PART OF AN ESCORT PROTECTING A CONVOY OF MERCHANT SHIPS HEADING FOR THE USSR.

IT'S ALWAYS NIGHT UP THERE, SO WE FOUGHT THE GERMANS IN THE DARK.

I WAS ON DUTY IN THE SHIPS MAGAZINE.

AND THAT'S WHERE I WAS WHEN WE CAME UNDER FIRE. I WAS LOCKED IN, THE ROOM SEALED TO PROTECT THE REST OF THE SHIP IF IT WAS HIT.

I COULD HEAR OUR GUNS RETURNING FIRE & THE BOYS ON DECK RUNNING ABOUT THE PLACE.

IF WE WERE HIT THERE'S NO DOUBT I'D KNOW ABOUT IT.

SURROUNDED AS I WAS BY A FEW HUNDRED TONNES OF GUN POWDER & EXPLOSIVES.

I WAS DOWN THERE FOR OVER TWELVE HOURS IN TOTAL

LISTENING, WAITING.

WHEN THE BATTLE WAS OVER I WAS CALLED TO THE BRIGDE. THE CAPTIAN GAVE ME SOME RUM.

WELL DONE WATTS.

HE SAID.

THE SCAR!

BY NATE HIGLEY!
© 2011 N. HIGLEY NATEHIGLEY.COM

I HAD EJECTED JUST IN TIME, BUT I HAD HURT MYSELF ON A ROUGH LANDING.

YEAH, BUT YOU'RE TOUGH PAW, I BET YOU BARELY FELT IT!

WELL, I LEARNED NOT TO LAND ON A MOUNTAIN SIDE EVER AGAIN —

SO I HEADED DOWN THE MOUNTAIN ROAD.

THEN I HEARD SOMETHING.

AGH!

OUT OF NOWHERE, I WAS STABBED IN THE GUT.

UGH!

I MANAGED TO GET IN A PUNCH.

WHOA...

I KNOCKED HIM OUT AND MANAGED TO FIND HELP. SO—THAT'S HOW I GOT **THE SCAR**!

HOLY CRAP!

20 SOME YEARS LATER...

AND THAT'S HOW HE SAID HE GOT HIS SCAR.

WHAT?

HE GOT THAT SCAR FROM HIS GALL BLADDER SURGERY!

AFTERWORD

SO GRANDPA CAME CLEAN AFTER GRANDMA TATTLED ON HIM. WHILE HE WAS IN THE AIR FORCE, HIS PLANE NEVER CRASHED. HIS EXCUSE FOR THE TALL TALE? FUN...

YOU'RE IN THE ARMY NOW!

A TRUE STORY BY AL FRANK

ART BY: SEAN DUFFIELD

STORYBOARD: AL FRANK

My father was a small framed guy most of his early life.

When he was in his twenties he was 5 foot 10, but weighed only about 125 lbs.

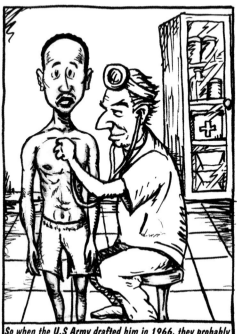

So when the U.S Army drafted him in 1966, they probably could have found a more perfect physical specimen.

Being a small guy, and having grown up in Chicago meant that he also had to fight a lot of bullies.

185.

He was sent to Fort Jackson in South Carolina for basic training. This was back during the days of segregation.

Nevertheless, they stuck him in a room with three beefy white guys. One day, one of the white boys got a letter.

It was a "Dear John" letter.

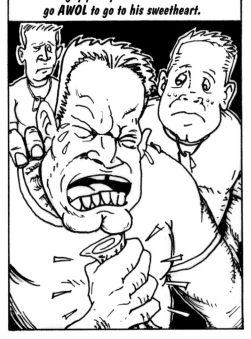

It hit the guy pretty hard. He threatened to go AWOL to go to his sweetheart.

Trying to be a nice guy, my father told him that it was a bad idea, that he'd get arrested and have to start basic training all over again.

This wasn't what the guy wanted to hear evidently, because he jumped on my father and started pounding him.

Where were the other two guys in the room? Well, they were egging on the guy who was beating on my old man.

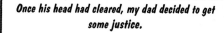

Once his head had cleared, my dad decided to get some justice.

He went to his Sergeant, who told him that there was nothing he could do. "Go tell it to the Chaplain!" he said.

The Chaplain was preaching the gospel of forgiveness, and turning the other cheek.

Finally, he went to the Company Commander, surely he could get justice from the head honcho!

Alas, it was not to be.

The Company Commander dismissed him by explaining that; "You're in the army now! Things don't always go the way you'd like them to. There's different people from different places..."

One thing you should know about my father, he's got a horrible (almost psychotic) temper, and he was now at the last straw.

The other black guys in the dorms offered to beat the shit out of the rednecks, but my father didn't want them getting into trouble on his account.

A few nights later, the rednecks came back to the dorm after a night of heavy drinking.

Hearing them coming up, my father formulated a plan.

He feigned sleep as the rednecks entered...

...And when he heard their snores, he made his move.

He put on his boots, and grabbed an entrenching tool from his locker.

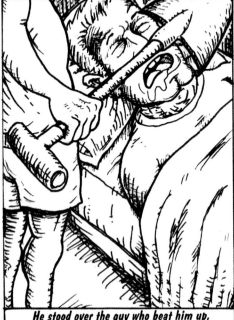

He stood over the guy who beat him up, listening to his snores...

... And smacked the guy right in the face!

With the lightning quickness of the wiry whippet, he smashes the shovel into face after bloody face.

Their screams rang out into the night.

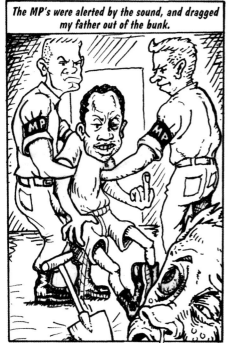

The MP's were alerted by the sound, and dragged my father out of the bunk.

They took him to the sergeant, who screamed with rage at my father.

But my father was calm, he didn't care anymore.

The company commander was woken up. He was livid with my father! He screamed:

WHAT THE HELL IS THE MATTER WITH YOU?!! ARE YOU **CRAZY?!!!**

My father was silent for a second, and then said:

Well, I'm in the army now! Things don't always go the way you want them to. There's different people from different places...

With that, the company commander let my father go without punishment! He knew there was nothing he could say.

HA HA!

The End

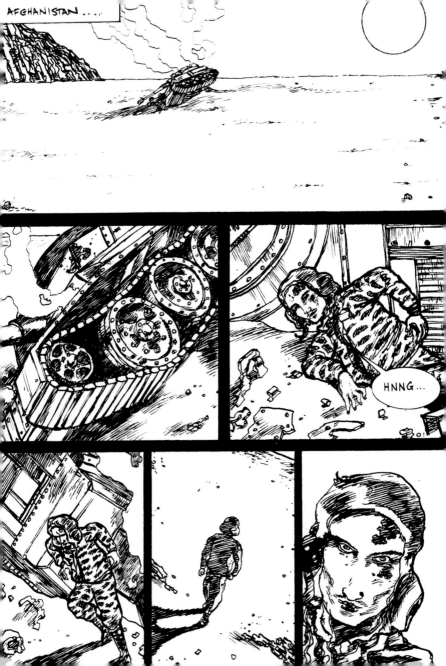

5 HOURS LATER...

TH.. THANK
GOD.. A TOWN.

196.

LIBERATION IN LIBERIA:

...OUR WOMEN'S STRUGGLE TO STOP A WAR & CHANGE A COUNTRY.

The war began here on Christmas Eve 1989... The start of terrible times...

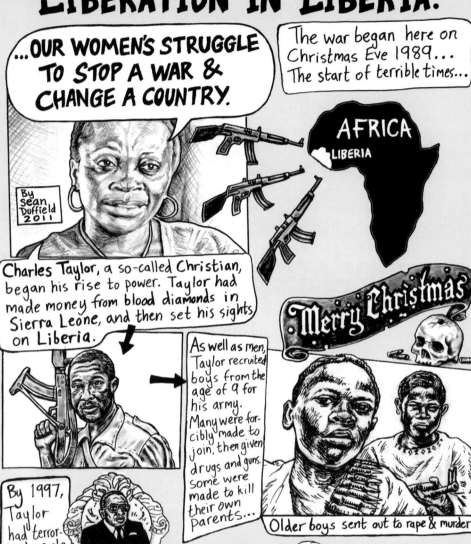

By Sean Duffield 2011

AFRICA
LIBERIA

Charles Taylor, a so-called Christian, began his rise to power. Taylor had made money from blood diamonds in Sierra Leone, and then set his sights on Liberia.

Merry Christmas

As well as men, Taylor recruited boys from the age of 9 for his army. Many were forcibly made to join, then given drugs and guns. Some were made to kill their own parents...

Older boys sent out to rape & murder.

By 1997, Taylor had terrorised people into voting him into power. He then went on to pocket Liberia's wealth & sell all it's resources to foreign companies

Meanwhile, more of our children were lost to murder, drugs, & brainwashing. & then they started killing each other...

198.

Rival warlords formed **L.U.R.D.** (Liberians United for Reconciliation & Democracy.) They fought against Taylor for control of the country.

But these rebels weren't liberating anyone. They recruited children too and sent them in to raid villages...

...Shooting people and hacking off limbs, just like Taylor's army.

The madness spread to my village. I fled with my family, but others didn't get away.

I remember finding a woman I knew, who was very traumatised & singing to herself. Her husband was lying decapitated next to her & her 12 year old daughter was in shock too.
Rebels had told the woman to sing, dance, & clap, whilst forcing her & the daughter to watch them decapitate the husband. Three men then raped her daughter in front of her, the daughter became pregnant from this rape.

Food became scarce for regular people. Taylor & the rebels ate while others starved, my two young children cried with hunger. It was not safe to go out and look for food, especially if you were a woman. I felt mostly fear and anger during that terrible time

199.

I wished my dead husband was alive to help and give me strength. I prayed to God that this madness would end, but I knew my faith alone was not enough...

Then one day at my church, some women from our nearby capital of Monrovia came to talk to us.

One of the speakers; Leymah Gbowee, had a dream about getting all the women of the Christian church together to stand up against war.

Another woman, Asatu Bah Kenneth a muslim, said how she had gone to Leyma's church to hear about her dream.

She was so moved by Leymah's ideas, that she'd pledged to talk to her muslim sisters so that the christian & muslim women could unite.

So began the Liberian womens' peace movement... Meanwhile, Charles Taylor announced:

Nobody will come out onto the streets to embarrass MY administration!

The women of the peace movement knew they might be killed, but were prepared to die for peace.

We knew that if Taylor was criticised directly, then he would have his special police kill us. Instead, the movement only focussed on calling for an end to war and rape.

We also had other means to get at the leaders on both sides. We pressured the priests to influence Taylor. We convinced some Imams to talk to the LURD leaders who were predominantly muslim. We tried pricking their consciences.

I joined the movement and travelled to Monrovia when I could. There were daily protests with thousands of women.

We all wore white, we carried banners, sang & protested. We felt strong. We grew in number. Taylor & the rebels tried to ignore us, but we wouldn't go away.

The soldiers were using sex as a weapon, so we used it as a tool too.

We encouraged women to deny their men sex if they fought in the war.

After a while, Taylor's men and LURD rebels would take turns showing up at the peace camps. They would try to scare and intimidate us. Sometimes they would attack us and we would run. But we didn't give up.

Eventually, Taylor couldn't avoid us any longer.

He agreed to see us. We were scared he might have us massacred as he had done with others who had spoken out.

WE ARE TIRED OF WAR. WE ARE TIRED OF RUNNING. WE ARE TIRED OF BEGGING FOR BULGAR WHEAT. WE ARE TIRED OF OUR CHILDREN BEING RAPED. WE ARE NOW TAKING THIS STAND TO SECURE THE FUTURE OF OUR CHILDREN...

We all sat on the ground as Leymah spoke for us. We held hands and prayed. It was a tense moment. You could hear the anger in Leymah's voice as she looked over at Charles Taylor.

He just sat there, silent, almost motionless as Leymah finished & handed over the unconditional proposal.

...BECAUSE ONE DAY, OUR CHILDREN WILL LOOK AT US & SAY; 'MAMA, WHAT WAS YOUR ROLE IN THE CRISIS?'

We wanted an immediate ceasefire, a dialogue for peace, and for Taylor to request UN intervention. To our surprise, he eventually agreed to go to peace talks in Ghana.

But the fighting didn't stop. Rebel warlords began invading the outskirts of Monrovia.

As the peace talks began, Taylor said he & his soldiers would fight to the death, whilst LURD leaders began planning their government positions.

The peace talks were deadlocked & became a joke. We knew some of our women must go to the talks or our work would be all for nothing. Luckily we found funders & 7 of our movement flew to Ghana.

Our 7 delegates then mobilised the Liberian women living in Ghana (most of whom were living in refugee camps). They travelled to the talks.

When the talks were in danger of breaking down, our women surrounded the hall and linked arms, preventing the peace talk delegates from leaving. Shockingly, a voice then came over the tannoy:

THE HALL HAS BEEN SEIZED BY GENERAL LEYMAH AND HER TROOPS!

We will not rest until we have peace.

Leymah told the people in the hall that our women wouldn't leave until the negotiators and warlords reached peace. The rebel leaders cursed at the women & tried to break out, to no avail.

Soldiers arrived and accused the women of 'obstructing justice', and said that they would arrest them all. On hearing this, Leymah boiled over; she cried out in desperate anger:

Yes, and I will make it VERY easy for you to arrest me! I will become naked! You leave me NO choice!

She started to strip off in front of the soldiers & delegates. In Africa, if an older woman gets angry at a man & exposes herself, it is said to be a powerful curse – a mother's curse. It is said to cause sickness, madness, or even death.

Ashamed at the desperate measures Leymah was taking, the war lords on both sides seemed to change for the first time. It was as if they realised they had gone too far, as though they had terribly offended their own mothers. The women, our women, had become their conscience.

From then on, the talks became sober and focussed. Taylor & the rebels stopped acting like boys and started acting like men. 2 of our women were allowed in the talks. 2 weeks later, peace was achieved.

Taylor agreed to step down & be exiled to Nigeria. A UN peacekeeping force entered Monrovia. A transitional govt. would lead to democratic elections.

It was a great time for us all, but we didn't stop there, we couldn't relent.

We made it clear we would watch the transistional govt closely. We encouraged fighters on both sides to surrender their weapons (the UN gave them cash). When eruptions started we calmed them.

HAND OVER OUR GUNS

WE LOVE YOU, DROP YOUR GUNS

We worked with child soldiers, those wounded & traumatised by war, as well as victims of rape. We also encouraged women to vote at the election.

In 2006, Ellen Johnson Sirleaf was elected Liberian president; the first ever woman president in Africa. I remember her opening declaration to us all...

I WANT TO GRATEFULLY ACKNOWLEDGE THE POWER OF OUR WOMEN FROM ALL WALKS OF LIFE...

...IT IS THE WOMEN WHO LABOURED & ADVOCATED FOR PEACE.

But she had inherited many problems.

The president introduced 6 women to the cabinet, which had previously been exclusively run by men. Corruption throughout gov--ernmental departments had been immense, and president Sirleaf tackled it head on.

People sought public positions because they could indulge in extortion. What we have done is to expose it.

She created much greater transparency and accountability, creating a strong anti-corruption campaign, which even caught out two members of the cabinet.

For the first time, women have a greater role in our society. I became a social worker, working with ex-child soldiers mainly. We create rehab--ilitation programs, like the amputee soccer team for example.

It has helped me overcome my anger at what these boys did. I now know how traumatised many are, and how many were hooked on heroin or cocaine, others riddled with guilt.

Another big problem our new government faced was rebuilding after the war. There was no mercy. American companies in Liberia were unwilling to give more to the country, saying they had an "understanding" with Taylor.

The US wouldn't cancel Liberia's debt either, until Sirleaf met with the Chinese president to speak about investment in Liberia's resources suddenly President Bush, scared that US comp--anies would lose out to China, cancelled Liberia's debt.

But now, due to the global financial crisis, Liberia has no money. Although there have been many positive changes, so many people still live in terrible poverty

Heroin, cocaine & aids are rife in the slums, as is prostitution; many of the sex workers lost their families in the war. Rape is on the increase again.

Sirleaf has enemies too. Old rebels and others who were loyal to Taylor, who never gave up their arms. The UN leaves Liberia this year, and some fear war and chaos will return.

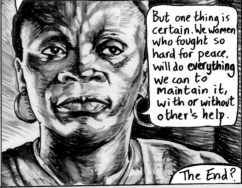

But one thing is certain. We women who fought so hard for peace, will do everything we can to maintain it, with or without other's help.

The End?

INKO PRESENTS
SEARCH & AVOID

When I arrived in Vietnam Black Power stuff was everywhere.

We did "Search and Avoid" patrols, just hangin' out in a nearby rubber plantation.

Based on a true story as recorded by
Dave Blalock in
"Ain't Marchin' Anymore: GIs Revolt in Vietnam".

We had an unofficial truce with the local Viet Cong that we wouldn't fuck with each other.

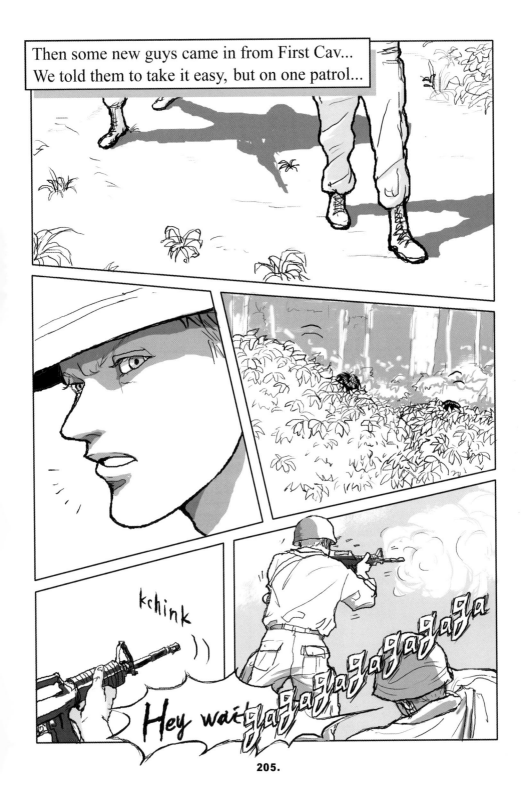

Then some new guys came in from First Cav...
We told them to take it easy, but on one patrol...

kchink

Hey wait

The officers had the scent of blood. The Company Commander started to put the pressure on...

We wanted to go back to "Search and Avoid", but they really started harassing people...

One night we all had a meeting on whether to frag the Company Commander. We decided to give him a warning...

What
the...

He went mad and
just intensified the shit
he was giving us.

So we left another grenade,
this time with the pin half out.

But he only got worse...

We had done our best to be reasonable.

One day he opened the door to his hooch.

None of us ever figured out who did it.

END

2007 ©Inko

MY 2 UNCLES

A TRUE STORY BY LAURA O'CALLAGHAN WHITE AND SEAN DUFFIELD
ARTWORK BY BEN JENNINGS

John with his first car

Bobby and his first car

My two uncles went to Vietnam. I wasn't born when they went there, therefore I didn't know what they were like before. My dad told me that as children they were inseparable. Dad didn't get drafted because, being the eldest brother, he'd already done national service before Vietnam When they went to war, my uncles were separated and had two very different roles.

One uncles job was to fly a plane and drop napalm on enemy targets. He didn't like what he had to do, but he was ordered... It had to be done.

They were both affected by what they had to do, but in different ways: My uncle who flew in the rescue chopper became self-destructive, taking up dangerous activities and acting recklessly. My uncle the napalm pilot b suffered with incredible, overwhelming guilt and depression... A lot of men who were drafted to Vietnam were treated like criminals when they came home, it was generally considered a "shameful" war. I don't think my uncles argued about it. I don't think they even spoke much about it. Certainly nobody was allowed to mention it. But the juxtaposition of experiences did seem to affect their relationship... one brother causing human destruction, while the other tried to salvage human life amidst the mess of conflict. As a result, they were never really close again.

As the Vietnam War dragged on, Richard Nixon became President in 1969.

THE TRUE OBJECTIVE OF THIS WAR IS *PEACE*. I'M GOING TO END THIS WAR, FAST. BUT IT MUST BE PEACE WITH *HONOR!*

Far from ending the war, Nixon expanded it. On April 30, 1970 he ordered U.S. troops to illegally invade Vietnam's neutral neighbor, Cambodia. It was the beginning of...

The End of the VIETNAM WAR

And a painful end it would be.

Announcing the invasion, Nixon told the nation...

IT IS NOT AMERICAN POWER, BUT OUR *WILL* AND *CHARACTER* THAT IS BEING TESTED TONIGHT.

On university campuses reaction was immediate. Even students who hadn't been part of the anti-war movement were outraged.

END THE WAR NOW

U.S. OUT OF CAMBODIA

PEACE NIXON IS A WAR CRIMINAL

Nixon's macho posturing only angered the protesters. Student strikes shut down campuses across the country.

Nixon drew the battle lines further when he was quoted calling protesters...

THESE *BUMS* YOU KNOW, BLOWING UP THE CAMPUSES.

When Vice President Spiro Agnew declared...

THE AUTHORITIES SHOULD IMAGINE THE STUDENTS ARE WEARING *BROWN SHIRTS* OR *WHITE SHEETS* AND ACT ACCORDINGLY.

...it just felt like something bad was going to happen.

Students at Kent State University in Ohio caused disturbances prompting the town's mayor to take action.

THERE ARE *OUTSIDE AGITATORS* IN KENT, BETTER CALL IN THE *NATIONAL GUARD.*

FROM THE BIG BOOK OF THE '70'S © JONATHAN VANKIN & STEVE MANNION. USED WITH PERMISSION OF DC COMICS.

THE MORNING OF MAY 4, ABOUT 200 STUDENTS GATHERED ON THE UNIVERSITY COMMONS. THE GUARD WAS THERE.

DURING THE DEMONSTRATION, SOME ANGRY STUDENTS THREW ROCKS AT THE GUARDSMEN.

SUDDENLY, WITHOUT WARNING— AND APPARENTLY WITHOUT ORDERS— THE NATIONAL GUARD FIRED.

BLAM! BLAM! BA-BLAM! BLAM!

THE NATIONAL GUARD KILLED FOUR STUDENTS THAT DAY AND WOUNDED NINE MORE. THE BRUTAL PRICE OF THE VIETNAM WAR HIT HOME--HARD.

NOT EVERYONE GOT IT. SOME PEOPLE EXPRESSED SUCH SENTIMENTS AS...

THE ONLY THING THE GUARD DID WRONG-- THEY DIDN'T KILL ALL OF THOSE PUNKS!

LONG-HAIRED TROUBLEMAKERS WHO USE BAD LANGUAGE SHOULD BE STOPPED!

BUT ON MAY 6, STUDENT "STRIKES" SHUT DOWN OVER 100 CAMPUSES. 80 PERCENT OF UNIVERSITIES HAD PROTESTS. 58 PERCENT OF THE STUDENTS WERE INVOLVED IN THEM, AND 75 PERCENT SUPPORTED THEM.

IF THEY WANT US TO MOVE, THEY'LL HAVE TO SHOOT US FIRST!

ON MAY 9, 120,000 PEOPLE DESCENDED ON WASHINGTON D.C. IN A MASSIVE ANTI-WAR DEMONSTRATION.

BY THE END OF 1970, POLLS SHOWED THAT ONLY 38 PERCENT OF AMERICANS SUPPORTED NIXON'S CONDUCT OF THE WAR, AN ALL-TIME LOW.

STOP WAR!

PRESSURED BY THE ANTI-WAR MOVEMENT, NIXON WITHDREW U.S. TROOPS BY THE THOUSANDS.

SEE YA STATESIDE, SUCKERS!

THAT MEANT FEWER U.S. CASUALTIES, TAKING THE STEAM OUT OF THE PROTESTS.

AMONG THE REMAINING TROOPS, MORALE DWINDLED AND DRUG ADDICTION BECAME AN EPIDEMIC. THE MILITARY ITSELF ESTIMATED THAT, IN 1970, 65,000 U.S. TROOPS WERE DRUG USERS.

ALSO IN 1970, THERE WERE OVER 2,000 REPORTED INCIDENTS OF "FRAGGING"— SOLDIERS KILLING THEIR OWN OFFICERS.

COME ON, MEN! LET'S GO GE-- HGGL!!

BLAM

DESPITE ALL INDICATIONS TO THE CONTRARY, THE WAR, AS FAR AS NIXON WAS CONCERNED, HAD A LONG WAY TO GO.

HE ORDERED DRAMATIC INCREASES IN BOMBING, KILLING TENS OF THOUSANDS OF VIETNAMESE.

AT THE SAME TIME, NIXON'S FOREIGN POLICY GURU HENRY KISSINGER WAS SECRETLY NEGOTIATING WITH VIETNAMESE COMMUNIST LEADER LE DUC THO IN PARIS.

IN APRIL, 1971, ANOTHER HUGE DEMONSTRATION— 300,000 STRONG— ENGULFED THE NATION'S CAPITAL.

THIS TIME, VIETNAM VETS PROTESTED, SYMBOLICALLY HURLING THEIR MEDALS AWAY.

IN THE SPRING OF 1971, AMERICANS HEARD THE GORY DETAILS OF THE 1968 MY LAI MASSACRE OF DOZENS OF VIETNAMESE CIVILIANS DURING THE TRIAL OF LIEUTENANT WILLIAM CALLEY.

THE LEAKED "PENTAGON PAPERS," PUBLISHED IN JUNE OF 1971, PROVED THAT THE GOVERNMENT HAD BEEN LYING FOR YEARS ABOUT U.S. INVOLVEMENT IN VIETNAM.

IMAGES OF "ORDINARY" AMERICAN BOYS COMMITTING UNSPEAKABLE ATROCITIES DEEPENED THE PUBLIC'S FAST-GROWING DISTASTE FOR THE NOW-LENGTHY WAR.

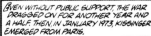

EVEN WITHOUT PUBLIC SUPPORT, THE WAR DRAGGED ON FOR ANOTHER YEAR AND A HALF. THEN, IN JANUARY 1973, KISSINGER EMERGED FROM PARIS.

WE HAVE ACHIEVED *PEACE* IN *VIETNAM!*

IT WAS A FUNNY KIND OF "PEACE." WAR IN VIETNAM RAGED ON FOR ANOTHER TWO YEARS. JUST WITHOUT AMERICANS.

ON APRIL 29, 1975, NORTH VIETNAMESE FORCES STORMED THE SOUTH VIETNAMESE CAPITAL OF SAIGON.

NO MATTER. BACK IN 1973, KISSINGER AND LE DUC THO WERE AWARDED THE NOBEL PEACE PRIZE. LE DUC THO DECLINED, SAYING...

I CANNOT ACCEPT BECAUSE THERE IS *NO PEACE* IN VIETNAM.

TO AMERICANS, THAT WAS JUST A MATTER OF SEMANTICS. THE SOLDIERS WERE COMING HOME. FINALLY, WE WERE *OUT OF THERE!*

WHEN NORTH VIETNAM RELEASED ITS 591 U.S. PRISONERS OF WAR, IT PROVIDED THE ONLY UPLIFTING SCENES OF THE ENTIRE, DECADE-LONG CONFLICT.

FOR MANY, THE WAR HAS NEVER ENDED. THEY MAINTAIN THAT MANY POWS *REMAIN* IN VIETNAM--THREE DECADES LATER, THEIR ALLEGED ABANDONMENT REMAINS, FOR SOME, A SYMBOL OF THE ENTIRE WAR.

POW/MIA
You are not forgotten

WE WON'T FORGET!

BUT MOST AMERICANS DID WANT TO FORGET. THEY WANTED TO FORGET THAT VIETNAM EVER HAPPENED.

VIET-*WHAT?* FORGET IT, MAN! LET'S GET *DOWN!*

THE "ME" DECADE WAS UNDER WAY.

BUT FORGETTING WAS IMPOSSIBLE. IMAGES OF LONELY, ALIENATED VETERANS HAUNTED AMERICA.

YOU TALKIN' TO ME?

THE VIETNAM WAR WOULD SHAPE THE SOCIETY FOR THE REST OF THE DECADE AND BEYOND.

IN 1991, FOLLOWING THE U.S. VICTORY IN THE ONE-SIDED WAR AGAINST IRAQ, PRESIDENT GEORGE BUSH DECLARED...

WE'VE FINALLY KICKED THAT *VIETNAM SYNDROME!!*

ONLY AN ORGY OF MILITARY VIOLENCE, APPARENTLY, COULD BANISH THOSE HORRIBLE MEMORIES.

THE QUIET OCCUPATION BY N. SCHULMAN

ON THE MORNING OF JUNE 13, 2002, SHIN HYO SOON AND SIM MI SUN WERE WALKING TO THEIR FRIEND'S BIRTHDAY PARTY IN THE TOWN OF EUIJEONGBU, SOUTH KOREA. THEY WOULD NOT MAKE IT THERE.

THE AMERICAN MILITARY CLAIMED IT WAS AN "ACCIDENT", THAT SERGEANTS MARK WALKER AND FERNANDO NINO OF THE SECOND INFANTRY DID NOT INTENTIONALLY RUN OVER THE TWO JUNIOR HIGH SCHOOL GIRLS WITH THEIR 50 TON ARMORED VEHICLE, CRUSHING THEM TO DEATH. THEY WERE EVENTUALLY CHARGED IN AN AMERICAN MILITARY COURT, BUT AS EXPECTED THEY WERE BOTH ACQUITTED OF NEGLIGENT HOMICIDE. THEY DID NOT HAVE TO FEAR ARREST OR PROSECUTION IN A SOUTH KOREAN COURT THANKS TO SOFA - THE STATUS OF FORCES AGREEMENT.

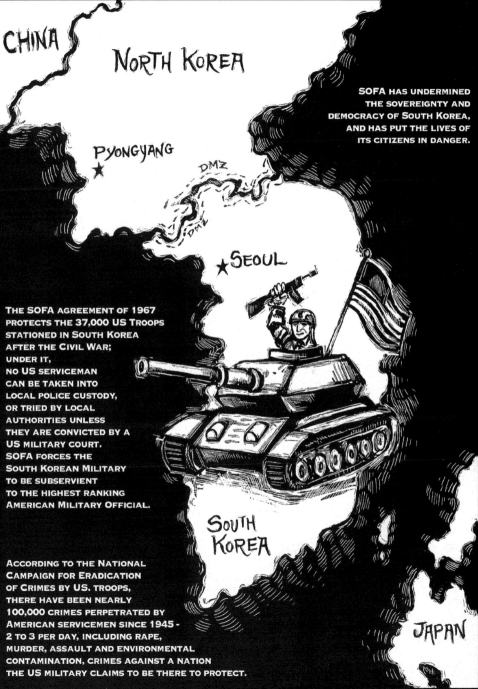

CHINA

NORTH KOREA

PYONGYANG
★

DMZ

DMZ

★ SEOUL

SOFA HAS UNDERMINED
THE SOVEREIGNTY AND
DEMOCRACY OF SOUTH KOREA,
AND HAS PUT THE LIVES OF
ITS CITIZENS IN DANGER.

THE SOFA AGREEMENT OF 1967
PROTECTS THE 37,000 US TROOPS
STATIONED IN SOUTH KOREA
AFTER THE CIVIL WAR;
UNDER IT,
NO US SERVICEMAN
CAN BE TAKEN INTO
LOCAL POLICE CUSTODY,
OR TRIED BY LOCAL
AUTHORITIES UNLESS
THEY ARE CONVICTED BY A
US MILITARY COURT.
SOFA FORCES THE
SOUTH KOREAN MILITARY
TO BE SUBSERVIENT
TO THE HIGHEST RANKING
AMERICAN MILITARY OFFICIAL.

SOUTH
KOREA

ACCORDING TO THE NATIONAL
CAMPAIGN FOR ERADICATION
OF CRIMES BY US. TROOPS,
THERE HAVE BEEN NEARLY
100,000 CRIMES PERPETRATED BY
AMERICAN SERVICEMEN SINCE 1945 -
2 TO 3 PER DAY, INCLUDING RAPE,
MURDER, ASSAULT AND ENVIRONMENTAL
CONTAMINATION, CRIMES AGAINST A NATION
THE US MILITARY CLAIMS TO BE THERE TO PROTECT.

JAPAN

THE MAJORITY OF VIOLENT CRIMES HAVE BEEN COMMITTED AGAINST WOMEN.

ONE PARTICULARLY HIDEOUS CRIME GALVANIZED RESISTANCE TO THE US. MILITARY PRESENCE: MS. YOON KUM-E WORKED AS A BAR GIRL IN A CLUB EXCLUSIVELY FOR US SERVICEMEN. SHE WENT HOME WITH PRIVATE KENNETH LEE MARKLE OF THE 125TH INFANTRY.

MARKLE BEAT MS. YOON UNCONSCIOUS, SHE WAS RAPED AND TORTURED TO DEATH.

THE CORONER FOUND TWO BROKEN BOTTLES INSIDE HER VAGINA, AND AN UMBRELLA HAD BEEN FORCED INTO HER RECTUM. SHE DIED FROM BLOOD LOSS.

220.

MS. JOON WAS ONE OF THOUSANDS OF WOMEN EMPLOYED IN THE "KIJICHON"-
GI TOWNS THAT HAVE DEVELOPED AROUND US. MILITARY BASES TO PROVIDE R & R.

MILITARY PROSTITUTION IS RAMPANT, AS IS THE ABUSE OF THE WOMEN WHO WORK
IN THE BARS AND CLUBS OF THE KIJICHON, MANY AGAINST THEIR WILL.

US. "COURTESY PATROLS" (MILITARY POLICE) PROVIDE SECURITY FOR SERVICEMEN
SOLICITING PROSTITUTES, MANY OF WHOM ARE TRAFFICKED WOMEN FROM EASTERN EUROPE,
THE PHILIPPINES AND SOUTH EAST ASIA. THESE WOMEN CAME TO SOUTH KOREA
LOOKING FOR LEGITIMATE WORK AND END UP IN GI TOWNS,
FORCED INTO PROSTITUTION, THEIR PASSPORTS TAKEN AWAY
BY BAR OWNERS AND INTIMIDATED BY THE
US. COURTESY PATROLS.

UNDER THE JAPANESE OCCUPATION,
WOMEN FORCED INTO SEXUAL SLAVERY
WERE CALLED "COMFORT WOMEN",
A LEGACY THAT HAS CONTINUED
UNDER THE AMERICAN MILITARY.

SOFA ALSO ALLOWS THE U.S. MILITARY
TO COMMIT ENVIRONMENTAL CRIMES IN SOUTH KOREA
WITH IMPUNITY. LIKE ON THE ISLAND OF VIEQUES,
THE AMERICAN MILITARY CONDUCTS TESTS IN THE SOUTHERN ISLANDS.
THE KOON-NI RANGE IS LESS THAN ONE MILE FROM LOCAL VILLAGES,
WHERE US F-16 JETS DROP DEPLETED URANIUM SHELLS.

THE NOISE AND POLLUTION ARE UNBEARABLE TO THE RESIDENTS
OF THESE FISHING VILLAGES. CANCER AND MISCARRIAGE RATES
GROW DISPROPORTIONATELY. UNDER SOFA, THE US. DOES NOT HAVE TO REVEAL
IF CHEMICAL OR BIOLOGICAL WEAPONS ARE HOUSED IN SOUTH KOREA,
OR WHAT ECOLOGICAL CONTAMINATION HAS ALREADY OCCURRED.

RESISTANCE IS GROWING TO THE AMERICAN MILITARY PRESENCE, AND WHAT IS SEEN AS THE DELIBERATE SABOTAGE OF PEACE TALKS BETWEEN NORTH AND SOUTH KOREA BY THE BUSH ADMINISTRATION.

ON NEW YEARS EVE, NEARLY ONE MILLION PEOPLE TOOK TO THE STREETS TO STAND UP AGAINST US MILITARISM, THE IMPENDING INVASION OF IRAQ AND ABOVE ALL, THE ACQUITTAL OF THE MURDERERS OF SHIN HYO SOON AND SIM MI SUN. PEOPLE FROM ALL WALKS OF LIFE CAME WITH THEIR CHILDREN TO RALLY OUT IN THE COLD FOR HOURS TO STAND FOR PEACE AND JUSTICE. DESPITE OFTEN VIOLENT REPRESSION FROM THE AUTHORITIES, THE CITIZENS OF SOUTH KOREA WILL CONTINUE TO FIGHT FOR AUTONOMY ON THE KOREAN PENINSULA.

DEDICATED TO THE MEMORY OF CHANG HYUN-OH SURVIVOR OF THE KOREAN WAR

223.

The poem "In Flander's Field" came to immortalize the poppy as a symbol of the Great War, but in the form of German resistance against the Nazi government, the second World War had it's own particular brand of--

Flower Power ✽
blumenkraft

Written by **GREG BALDINO**   Illustrated by **NOELLE BARBY**
Lettering by NATE HIGLEY

In Berlin, the shoots began to push through the concrete appropriately on Rose Street...

As the war began Jewish men with German wives were spared deportment to the concentration camps. But in early 1943, a final roundup called the Fabrikaktion began gathering up those remaining men, most of whom held factory jobs.

Before being sent on the trains, they were held at Rosenstrasse 2-4. In late February, their wives began to gather in front of the building, demanding the release of their husbands. Within a day, they filled the street.

The SS division in charge of the action tried to deter them with gunfire, but after scattering, the women would always return. This continued for a week.

The SS guards could handle sending Jewish citizens to their death but they couldn't handle a street thick with "Aryan" Germans begging for them back and the men were released from their "Rose Street" holding center.

[1] Let our husband's go! [2] Clear the street!

For girls in Germany under Nazi rule, there was only the *Bund Deutscher Madel*, mandatory youth indoctrination to grow up and give birth to the next

generation of soldiers. Sophia Scholl had other aspirations.

Coming from a dissenting Lutheran family, Scholl saw the Nazi ideology as poison, even as a girl in the BDM.

At the University of Munich, she studied philosophy, and joined The White Rose, an underground group of pamphleteers. While tossing pamphlets condemning the Nazi regime off a gymnasium balcony, she was spotted by a janitor. She and her comrades were caught, found guilty of treason, and executed by guillotine.

SHE WAS TWENTY-TWO.

But not every story of resistance (and there were many) had such a terrible end. When the Nazis banned the German Youth Movement, replacing it with the Hitler-Jugend, not everyone took it lying down.

There was no central group, instead cells of *Edelweisspiraten* turned up everywhere throughout Germany. They lived free, scrapped with Hitler Youth, and when the war began acted as saboteurs and aided deserters.

Many left school before they could be drafted, and took to calling themselves Edelweiss Pirates, after a mountain flower long associated with courage and adventure.

Despite the Gestapo's best efforts, the Pirates were never quelled and few were caught.

In their numbers the most delicate flowers can crack the firmaments of evil with their roots. For each resistance group they put down, yet another would spring up. Fear and hate proved ultimately no match for love and hope.

FAR, FAR AWAY ON THE EDGE OF SOMEWHERE VERY COLD LIVED A WHOLE BUNCH OF LINEAR ANIMALS.

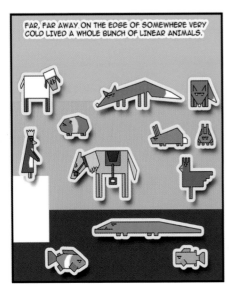

THEY'D GAMBOL AND PLAY, AND GENERALLY RUN ABOUT IN STRAIGHT LINES TO THEIR HEART'S CONTENT.

THERE WERE SHARP CORNERS AS FAR AS THE EYE COULD SEE, AT ALL ANGLES OF INCIDENCE.

OVER A COUPLE OF MONTHS, NEWS BEGAN TO FILTER THROUGH ON THE POINTY RADIO OF A DISTANT LAND WHERE A PARTICULARLY NASTY ANIMAL WAS IN CHARGE, AND HAD SET ABOUT SYSTEMATICALLY BITING ANYONE HE DIDN'T LIKE!

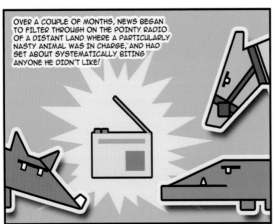

THE LINEAR ANIMALS THOUGHT IT SOUNDED PRETTY BAD AND POSTED OFF SEVERAL SQUARE CANS OF FOOD IN SUPPORT.

NOTHING MUCH HAPPENED FOR A WHILE...

THEN, ONE DAY, A NEW ARRIVAL APPEARED IN LINEAR LAND.

HERE HE COMES!

HE WAS A BADGER LIKE ANY OTHER BADGER EXCEPT...

...HE WAS ROUND *!?!*

HE ALSO SPOKE IN A STRANGE WAVY WAY AND LIKED TO EAT WORMS WITH CURVES.

THE LINEAR CREATURES FOUND OUT THAT THE EMPEROR PENGUIN HAD DECREED THAT THE ROUND BADGERS WERE TO BE RE-HOUSED IN LINEAR LAND AS THEY WERE IN DANGER OF BEING BITTEN, AND IT WOULD MAKE HIM LOOK GOOD.

AT FIRST, THERE WERE ONE OR TWO ROUND BADGERS...

...BUT MORE AND MORE APPEARED UNTIL THE LINEAR ANIMALS BEGAN TO GET CONCERNED!

NOBODY KNEW WHAT THE BADGERS WERE SAYING AND THEY ALL KEPT HANGING AROUND IN GROUPS WITH NOTHING TO DO, AS THE EMPEROR HAD ALSO DECREED THAT THE BADGERS WEREN'T ALLOWED TO DO ANYTHING.

MR AND MRS FERRET WERE VERY ANNOYED BECAUSE THEY COULD SEE THE BADGERS FROM THEIR FERRET HOLE –

– MOOCHING ABOUT IN CIRCLES AND NOT BEING STRAIGHT AT ALL.

THE EMPEROR HAD ALSO STARTED IMPORTING CURVY WORMS ESPECIALLY FOR THE BADGERS...

...AND RUMOURS WERE FLYING AROUND THAT THE BADGERS WERE BEING GIVEN MOBILE PHONES.

'MOBILE PHONES!', EXCLAIMED MRS FERRET, 'THEY SHOULD BE GIVING THOSE TO THE STARVING LINEAR WEASELS UP THE ROAD THAT I'D SUCCESSFULLY IGNORED UNTIL IT BECAME CONVENIENT TO REMEMBER THEM!'

THE LINEAR CREATURES BLAMED THE BADGERS FOR THE BAD WEATHER...

...THE FLAT TYRE ON THE BUS...

...AND THE WINDOW THAT JUNIOR GUINEA-PIG HAD PUT THROUGH BEFORE HE GOT EATEN IN AN EARLIER EPISODE.

230.

THE BADGERS TRIED EVERYTHING, EVEN WORKING WITH A LINEAR BADGER INTERPRETER TO SHOW THAT THEY MEANT NO HARM AND WERE PLEASED TO BE THERE EVEN IF NOBODY LIKED THEM, BUT IT WAS TO NO AVAIL.

THE NEWSPAPERS PUT PRESSURE ON THE EMPEROR TO SEND THE BADGERS BACK...

...WHICH HE DID, BECAUSE IT MADE HIM LOOK GOOD.

WHETHER THEY GOT BITTEN OR NOT, NOBODY CARED.

YEARS LATER, WHEN THE LAND WAS NICE AND LINEAR AGAIN, MR MOLE WAS DIGGING ABOUT IN THE SOIL WHEN HE DUG UP A ROUND BOOK.

IT TOLD THE STORY OF HOW, LONG AGO, THE ORIGINAL CIRCULAR OCCUPANTS OF LINEAR LAND HAD DIED OUT WHEN ODD-LOOKING ANIMALS WITH STRAIGHT EDGES HAD INVADED AND BITTEN THEM.

AND THE MOON SHONE BRIGHTLY, IN THE DEEP PRUSSIAN BLUE SKY OF LINEAR LAND...

...FAR, FAR AWAY ON THE EDGE OF SOMEWHERE VERY COLD,

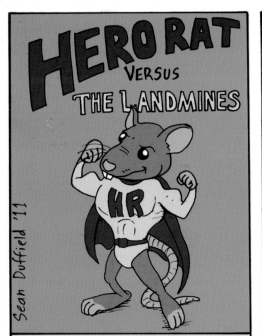

HERO RAT VERSUS THE LANDMINES

Sean Duffield '11

This is the story of a special kind of rat: The African Pouched Rat.

A lot of people think of rats as vicious, disease carrying vermin, but oh no, not these fellas...

I'M SO MISUNDERSTOOD!

These little critters have a gift that helps get rid of landmines.

The idea to use the rats to clear landmines came about at the end of Mozambique's civil war. Bart Weetjens, a Dutch buddhist & social entrepreneur, realised that rats are highly intelligent animals, & could be trained to detect mines. He set up APOPO; a landmine detection development, so that Mozambique's communities could be rid of the destructive munitions, children could play safely, and land could be reclaimed, allowing the country to move on and develop. Apopo began training local people to handle & train the rats, and to go out into the dangerous heavily mined areas.

Their super-olfactory senses give them the ability to sniff out landmines easily.

SNIFF SNIFF!

They also have the ability of being able to smell out Tuberculosis in sputum samples, evaluating up to 40 samples in 7 minutes, equal to what a skilled lab technician using microscopy would test in a whole day, and at a fraction of the cost.

232.

... And they are not heavy enough to trip a mine and so are quite safe.

WHAT YOU GONNA DO MINE, HUH?

WHAT YOU GONNA DO?

BOINGA! BOINGA!

They also do not bond to just a single trainer, nor are they prone to ennui like sniffer dogs are.

I MEAN, WHAT'S MY MOTIVATION? IT'S NEVER BEEN THE SAME SINCE ERIC LEFT...

GOD I MISS HIM...

But, the two are complimentary allies.

The rats only cost 6000 euros to train, roughly a third of what it costs to train a mine detection dog.

ALL IN A DAY'S WORK!

... And you could say they work for peanuts.

Gradually, people are learning to take this little rodent seriously in the fight against landmines.

HERO RATS! WE NEED YOU!

From 2008-2010, about 30 Hero Rats covered over 1·8 million square metres of Mozambican land with their trainers, ferreting out over 570 mines, 181 unexploded ordnance and 3871 small arms...

DE-ACTIVATED LANDMINES

A JOB WELL DONE IF I SAY SO MYSELF!

IT'S A DIRTY JOB, BUT SOMEONE'S GOT TO DO IT!

That land is now safe for public use, benefitting nearly 44,500 people!

THANK YOU HERO RAT!

DON'T MENTION IT!

But millions of mines still need to be cleared throughout Africa. The Hero Rats still have a lot of work to do!

APOPO has an 'Adopt-A-Rat' program for only 5 euros a month, or a one-off payment of 60 euros (around £50).

...AND DON'T FORGET, HERO RATS FIGHT AGAINST T.B. TOO!

To help, or to find out more about how the Hero Rats program works, go to www.herorat.org   THE END!

WAR CRIMINALS

STORY: SEAN DUFFIELD   ART: CLIODHNA

AND HOW'S THIS FOR IRONY; IN THE SAME WEEK THAT RIGHT-WINGERS WERE CALLING FOR THE ARREST AND ASSASSINATION OF THE HEAD OF WIKILEAKS FOR LEAKING THE TRUTH ABOUT CORRUPTION AND WAR CRIMES...

HUNT HIM DOWN LIKE A TERRORIST

IT'S TREASON ..EXECUTE HIM!

...A PROPOSAL WAS ALSO ANNOUNCED UNDER THE UK POLICE REFORM BILL WHICH WILL MAKE IT MUCH MORE DIFFICULT TO OBTAIN AN ARREST WARRANT FOR ANYONE ACCUSED OF WAR CRIMES AND CRIMES AGAINST HUMANITY.

BUT YOU MUST ARREST HIM, HE'S RESPONSIBLE FOR GENOCIDE, TORTURE, ASSASSINATING POLITICAL RIVALS

YES, BUT YOU'D WANT HIM ON YOUR SIDE WOULDN'T YOU? AND HE DID TORTURE ALL THOSE TERRORIST SUSPECTS FOR US

IF PASSED THE NEW LEGISLATIONS WOULD ALLOW THE DIRECTOR OF PUBLIC PROSECUTIONS, WHO IS APPOINTED AND "SUPERINTENDED" BY A GOVERNMENT MINISTER, THE ATTORNEY GENERAL, TO HAVE A VETO OVER WHETHER A SUSPECTED WAR CRIMINAL IS TO BE ARRESTED, NO MATTER HOW CLEAR THE EVIDENCE.

THE DPP COULD FIND THEMSELVES UNDER IMMENSE PRESSURE FROM THEIR BOSS, THE ATTORNEY GENERAL, TO REFUSE AN ARREST WARRANT APPLICATION IF IT WAS FOR SOMEONE FROM WHAT THE GOVERNMENT CONSIDERED AN 'ALLY' COUNTRY.

THERE'S NOTHING TO SEE HERE

IT SEEMS THAT 'FREE AND DEMOCRATIC' BRITAIN AND THE U.S. ARE FRIENDS AND HOST TO A LOT OF WAR CRIMINALS THESE DAYS...IT MAKES ME THINK OF A CERTAIN CHARACTER FROM A KUBRICK MOVIE...

YES MEIN FUHRER!... I MEAN MR PRESIDENT

SLOWPOKE

*MEDIUM ALTITUDE LONG ENDURANCE (ACTUAL TERMINOLOGY!)

Desensitise the heart, dumb down the mind. Fill the vision with edited images, but keep the third-eye blind. Stuff the body full of junk, learn who to despise. Technology's seduction to allure and hypnotise. Stay in a state of denial and fear, join others in mass confusion. Make sure dissent is squashed & drowned, to maintain corruption's illusion; That this way is the best, normal, necessary & healthy. **Where the poor take the brunt of it, and the greedy get more wealthy**

IT'S RAINING - DAMN. THAT'LL MEAN A SMALLER TURN OUT AT THE DEMOSTRATION...

THE B.C. LIBERAL GOVERMENT HAS DECLARED A TAKE-NO-PRISONERS SCORTCHED-EARTH CLASS WAR ON ITS ENEMIES: THE POOR, NURSES, TEACHERS, STUDENTS, WORKERS, UNIONS, FIRST NATIONS, WOMEN, HANDICAPPED... BASICALLY, ANYONE NOT RICH.

I DRESS IN LEATHER AND STEEL-TOED BOOTS TO PROTECT MYSELF. I LEAVE MY BAG AT HOME IN CASE I HAVE TO DODGE POLICE ATTACKS. GAS, PEPPER SPRAY CLUBS.

THESE FANATICAL FREE-MARKET TALIBAN ARE SLASHING BUDGETS, MEDICARE, EDUCATION, WRECKING THE PUBLIC SECTOR TO SELL THE ASSETS OF THE PROVINCE CHEAP TO THE WEALTHY PATRONS WHO BANKROLLED THEIR ELECTION.

IT'S THE POLICE WHO DECIDE IF A DEMONSTRATION TURNS VIOLENT AND YOU NEVER KNOW WHEN IT MIGHT SUIT THEIR PURPOSES.

SLASHING TAXES FOR THE RICH CORPORATE WELFARE BUMS WHILE RAISING TAXES ON THE POOR. THE LIBERALS HAVE TURNED A REVENUE SURPLUS INTO A HUGE DEBT.

"THE PEOPLE, UNITED..."

BARS ARE OVERFLOWING WITH PEOPLE WATCHING THE OLYMPIC MEN'S SEMI-FINAL HOCKEY GAME. CANADA VS BELARUS.

CIRCUS'S WIN EVERY TIME...

AT THE WESTIN BAYSHORE HOTEL THE LIBERAL CABINET IS BEING WINED AND DINED BY THE ONLY PEOPLE THEY TRULY REPRESENT, THE PARASITES OF THE CHAMBER OF COMMERCE. EVERYONE ELSE IS A "SPECIAL INTEREST GROUP".

OUTSIDE, SEVERAL HUNDRED OF THE USUAL SUSPECTS ARE GETTING SOAKED IN THE RAIN.

= YOUNG ANARCHO-PUNKS, AGING RADICALS, NATIVES, SENIORS, BUS RIDERS, ASSORTED ODDBALLS, SENIORS, THE UNEMPLOYED AND THE UNEMPLOYABLE. THE MOOD IS SURPRISINGLY CHEERFUL AS OLD FRIENDS MEET. DEMONSTRATIONS FOR SOME ARE SOCIAL EVENTS.

WHERE ARE THE UNIONS?

I'M HANDED LEAFLETS AND EARPLUGS.

I KNOW NOBODY; MY "COMRADES" HAVN'T SHOWN UP. BRYCE LIKELY FORGOT AND I SUSPECT STEVE'S WATCHING THE HOCKEY GAME.

THE OTHER PROTESTORS LOOK AT ME LIKE I'M A NARC.

I WANDER AROUND THE EDGES OF THE CROWD, OBSERVING THE ACTION IN A DETACHED WAY. I FIND IT SO HARD TO JOIN IN.

I WISH I'D THOUGHT TO BRING A POT OR PAN TO BANG ON.

I CAN'T GET INTO THE CHANTING, IT'S EMABRASSING, THOSE FEEBLE CLICHES STRANGLE IN MY THROAT.

THE PEOPLE, UNITED, WILL NEVER BE DEFEATED! THE P U

THE PEOPLE, UNITED, ARE WATCHING THE HOCKEY GAME...

243.

I'M COLD AND WET, THERE'S A TABLE SERVING SOME VEGAN MUCK BUT I NEED PROPER TEA, NOT SOME HIPPY HERBAL PISS-WATER!

HAVE YOU SEEN...?

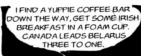

I FIND A YUPPIE COFFEE BAR DOWN THE WAY, GET SOME IRISH BREAKFAST IN A FOAM CUP. CANADA LEADS BELARUS THREE TO ONE.

I PENATRATE AN UNPROTECTED SECTOR OF THE POLICE LINES TO SIT IN A WATERPARK AND SIP MY TEA. I'M CAREFUL NOT TO TROD ON THE PLANTS.

NOBODY TAKES ANY NOTICE.

I REST MY FEET. MY ACHILLES TENDONS ARE STILL SWOLLEN FROM A FOUR MONTH TRANSIT STRIKE HALF A YEAR AGO THAT TRANSLINK ARRANGED TO SAVE MONEY SO THEY COULD BUILD MORE SKYTRAIN.

I PROTESTED THAT TOO.

NO MATTER HOW FURIOUS I GET IN PRIVATE AT ALL THIS INJUSTICE I CANNOT EASILY EXPRESS MY ANGER IN PUBLIC. I'M AFRAID I MIGHT LOSE CONTROL...

STORY OF MY LIFE...

SHIT, WHAT AM I DOING HERE?

THE PROTEST IS BREAKING UP, PEOPLE ARE GOING HOME.

MY LEGS ARE GOING NUMB. IT'S TIME TO GO BOOKSHOPPING...

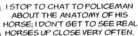

I STOP TO CHAT TO POLICEMAN ABOUT THE ANATOMY OF HIS HORSE; I DON'T GET TO SEE REAL HORSES UP CLOSE VERY OFTEN.

BELOW THAT THE LEGS ALL BONE...

I ASK A COP IF I CAN THROW AWAY MY EMPTY CUP IN THE BIN BY THE HOTEL ENTRANCE, HE TELLS ME TO LEAVE IT IN THE PLANTER FOR THE HOTEL STAFF TO CLEAN UP.

I HATE TO LITTER.

I WALK ALONG THE SEAWALL TOWARDS DOWNTOWN, PAST THE SILENT YUPPIE CONDO'S, SUDDENLY ALONE...

SIGH... IT'S SUCH A PITY; THIS COULD BE SUCH A COOL PLACE TO LIVE. FOR ALL OF US...

IT'S CLEAR NOW WHAT THE LAST TWENTY-FIVE YEARS OF BULLSHIT HAVE REALLY BEEN ABOUT, ALL THOSE YEARS OF RESTRAINT...

...CUTBACKS, DOWNSIZING, RATIONALIZATIONS, RIGHTSIZING, PROPER FISCAL MANAGEMENT, LIVING WITHIN OUR MEANS, BALANCED BUDGETS, LAYOFFS, COMPETIVENESS, PAYING DOWN THE DEBT, BELT-TIGHTENING, SHORT-TERM PAIN, REFORM, ECONOMIC THEORY, FREE MARKETS, ALL THE LIES...

IT'S ALWAYS BEEN ABOUT ONE THING, MORE MONEY FOR THE RICH AND NOTHING MORE.

MY ADVICE? BE RICH KIDS. LIE, CHEAT, STEAL, SELL DRUGS, PIMP YOUR MOTHERS ASS IF YOU HAVE TO BUT BY ANY MEANS, NESSACCARY BE RICH!

THE PEOPLE, UNITED, ARE FUCKED.

BECAUSE BEING RICH IS ALL THAT MATTERS. IF YOU'RE NOT RICH YOU ARE NOTHING.

THE BCTV (THE PROPAGANDA WING OF THE LIBERAL PARTY) NIGHTLY NEWS PORTRAYED OUR PEACEFUL PROTEST WAS AS A RABID LYNCH MOB.

THE NEXT DAY IN VICTORIA AT A UNION ORGANIZED RALLY 20,000 TO 40,000 PEOPLE MARCHED AGAINST THE CUTS. THE "FREE PRESS" VIRTUALLY IGNORED THE EVENT, LIKE IT MEANT NOTHING.

THE CANADIAN MEN'S AND WOMEN'S HOCKEY TEAMS WENT ON TO WIN THE OLYMPIC GOLD MEDALS.

HOORAY...

COLIN UPTON 2

245.

"If The Law And Police Can't Do Anything, It's About Time Someone Else Did":
The SMASH EDO campaign to close down an arms factory, and the shameful History of ITT

This is the true story of the long and ongoing struggles between an arms component factory in Brighton UK, and those who are committed to shutting it down. The factory; EDO MBM/ ITT, and dedicated anti-war protesters have been involved in a couple of landmark court cases, the latest occurring in 2010 after six protesters broke-in and 'decommissioned' the factory in the previous year, causing over £300,000 worth of damage and preventing the manufacture of parts for several weeks.

The decommissioning took place on the night of January 17th 2009 whilst the bombings of Gaza were occurring, this being the reason why the campaigners planned to smash up the arms making equipment that day. They did not see the the act of destroying equipment that is used to kill people as violent or a crime, particularly when it was being used in greater crimes. The 6 people knew that the factory made bomb release components that were being used specifically by Israeli aircraft in the bombing of innocent civilians, and that no-one else was willing to stop that.

This story is one that many people don't know, and if they do hear about it in the national press, then it is often from the same jaded, skewed Murdoch press style news angle where the factory is shown as respectably British; how the company is 'good for Britain's economy' or has 'created jobs for British people', and the protesters are smeared and written off as radicals, law breakers, or, more recently, accused of anti-semitism. But the full story regarding the factory and the company who own it, is a lot deeper, darker and more disturbing than the public have been led to believe, and during the case the protesters' true motives, and reasons for entering the factory became apparent.

Knowing that there was a possibility that they may face jail as a result of following their conscience and doing what the law, the council and politicians would not, the protesters filmed their personal and political reasons and intentions for going into the factory prior to entering, and after destroying the equipment they voluntarily waited for the police to come and arrest them. You can see their video statements on youtube by typing in "Plan to Smash EDO Brighton"

At the time that the defendants made the video, official reports were saying 350 children were killed in Gaza, that families who left their homes and took flight to the UN compound were still targetted, the warehouses that were full of humanitarian aid were bombed. As the protesters knew that a factory on their doorstep was selling components to the Israeli airforce, they felt they had to do something.

This story is also about the company who now own this factory; ITT, a US based multi-national which has untold blood on it's hands and a history of deceit; of not only covertly conspiring and orchestrating situations that were crucial to some of the world's most ruthless dictators gaining power, but then knowingly propping up those genocidal regimes, so that the company could enjoy making 'a healthy buck' (or rather billions).

ITT is a company who have very powerful political friends, and excellent PR and lobbying departments, who help to whitewash over their past and presents deeds.

This same company, has denied claims that it's Brighton factory makes computerised arms components and circuit boards for F-16 fighter jets, but due to the Smash Edo campaign, all that has changed, and the truth came to light in court.

A Quick History Of The Smash Edo Campaign.

The Smash Edo campaign emerged from the marches against the war on Iraq. When Brighton residents discovered a local company was profiteering from, and helping make possible the slaughter of innocent civilians in Iraq, Afghanistan, Palestine & Lebanon, then many decided to act. Campaigners include students, quakers, buddhists, anti-war activists and other concerned citizens who united under the 'Smash EDO' banner.

The Brighton factory located on Home Farm Industrial Estate, is part of EDO MBM Technology Lt which is now a unit of ITT Integrated Structures and was previously owned by EDO Corp, USA. It produces bomb racks, release units, and arming mechanisms which turn planes into war fight-

-ers and bombers. The factory has produced, amongst many other things, parts of the Paveway laser-guided bombs which were the most used weapon in operation "Shock & Awe"; the sustained bombardment and mass slaughter of civilians in Iraq over a number of days. They also own the manufacturing rights to three components for the Israeli F16; the trigger unit, the release unit and the bomb rack.

There have been numerous protests and direct actions since 2004 voicing the opinion that the corporation should close or convert its factory to civilian use. Protest actions have included road blockades, rooftop occupations, noise demos, comedy protests, attempted weapons inspections and three peace camps set up in woodland next to the factory. There have also been several marches through Brighton city centre involving thousands of protesters.

When the protests started in April 2004, EDO MBM complained of harrassment and under advice of Sussex Police, sought an injuction order under the 1997 Prevention of Harrasment Act. This law, originally created to protect members of the public from stalkers, was now being used to protect an arms corporation from criticism or public dissent. EDO hired a specialist ex-military solicitor, and with the aid of the police, they attempted to make protesting almost completely illegal for over a mile and a half radius surrounding the factory. This PHA act, had been used in this way 20 times by the same lawyer against Animal Rights campainers, but this was the first time a non-animal rights group had been targetted. If EDO had won, this would have meant that other arms companies who were involved in immoral acts and illegal activities could have used the same law to avoid accountability, while civil liberties and the right to protest would have been greatly depleted.

The protesters defended themselves, and had they lost, they would have been saddled with the factory's legal costs; potentially millions of pounds. They decided to mount a defence in the high court demanding the right to protest. A year long court battle ensued, which ended in EDO losing and having to pay $1 million in legal costs, as well as EDO corp losing $2.7 million in profits that year. The factory's Managing Director of that time, David Jones, then resigned - This was the first major victory for the campaign.

During this first year of protests EDO MBM removed the info that it was making components for VER-2 bomb racks for Israeli F-16's from it's websites but continued to produce them (They deny this). The website still continues to advertise the ERU-151 Ejector Release Unit and the zero-retention force arming unit, even though two of it's Managing Directors, David Jones and Paul Hills, denied this fact under oath saying that it had never been made.

The company has also been described by the government as filling out it's export applications in an 'unconventional' way, which some have claimed is to escape the scrutiny of arms export controls. This all came to light under the Smash EDO court cases, which also begs the question; what are other UK arms companies getting away with who haven't been exposed in court?

In 2009, prior to the decommissioning, Brighton Green party councillors showed their support for the Smash EDO campaigners, by proposing a motion which condemned the activities of EDO/ITT, and acknowledged the link between the factory's components and F16's using them in Gaza, and asked that the factory's facilities be used to produce non-military components. This motion was refused by the City Council convenor, the reason given that it was 'not directly related to Brighton'.

This of course turned out to be untrue.

MAYDAY! MAYDAY!

MASS STREET PARTY

AGAINST WAR AND GREED

About ITT: A History Of Deceit & Supporting Genocidal Regimes.

In December 2007, EDO MBM was bought out by ITT, one of the biggest arms manufacturers in the world, who now own the Brighton factory.

ITT has an incredibly dark history, of supporting fascism and putting profit before ethics and human lives.

ITT & HITLER: ITT, a US based company, did business with the nazi regime in a multiple of ways prior to, and throughout WW2. Key companies that maintained the German telephone network were ITT subsidiaries at that time, and communications were obviously of strategic importance for Nazi Germany. ITT subsidiaries produced vital supplies such as switchboards, telephones, teleprinters, aircraft intercoms, submarine and ship phones, electric buoys, alarm gongs, air raid warning devices, radar equipment, radio parts and 30,000 fuses per month for artillery shells used to kill allied troops. But the most shocking is yet to come.

ITT also profitted from the bombing of London and south-east England as its German subsidiary Focke-Wulfe built the "FW 191 heavy bomber" and the "FW 190D fighter bomber". By 1943 13% of ITT's income was generated from Nazi Germany.

Numerous payments were made to Heinrich Himmler in the late 1930s throughout World War II itself via ITT German subsidiaries. The first meeting between Hitler and ITT was reported in August 1933, when the U.S. based CEO Sosthenes Behn, and I.T.T. German representative Henry Manne met with Hitler in Berchesgaden. Subsequently, Behn made contact with the Secretary of State Keppler and, through Keppler's influence, Nazi banker Baron Kurt von Schröder became the guardian of ITT interests in Germany. Schröder acted as the conduit for ITT money funnelled to Heinrich Himmler's S.S. organization in 1944.

At the time of the Pearl Harbour attack in 1941, ITT's investments in Nazi Germany totalled $30 million. They continued to invest in and collaborate with Nazi Germany after the USA entered the war, in fact striking a deal with Hitler ensuring that the Nazi government would not acquire ITT's shares, but would be responsible for the administration of the shares. ITT literally went into partnership with the Nazi government in wartime.

ITT later sued the American government, receiving $27 million for damage that had been inflicted on their German plants by Allied bombers, despite the fact that these factories were building Nazi military equipment to attack the allies during the war.

ITT & FRANCO: To protect the interests of its Spanish subsidiary the Compania Telefonica Nacional de Espana (CTNE), which held a monopoly over Spain's telephone system, ITT actively supported fascist dictator General Franco's rise to power while opposition to ITT's presence and profiteering in Spain grew. Sosthenes Behn provided private phone links between the plotters at Madrid, and Generals Francisco Franco and Emilio Mola in the provinces. Behn's activities allowed the extremely effective coordination between Franco's widely scattered leaders in the early days of the Spanish Civil War. CTNE technicians were also repairing damaged telephone equipment for Franco's insurgents. The US government claimed neutrality in the Spanish civil war, but failed to prevent US companies like ITT financing and supporting Franco. It was this extra support which won Franco the war, and resulted in 36 years of fascist rule in Spain.

ITT & PINOCHET: In 1970 ITT tried to get the CIA to support the right-wing opponent of Salvadore Allende for the presidency in Chile. ITT offered to pay the CIA $1million towards their campaign against Allende. Allende was campaigning on a platform of ending corruption and planned to expropriate American businesses, including ITT, to nationalise Chile's industries so that it's people would no longer be exploited by U.S. companies.

In October, 1971, President Allende, the first democratically elected socialist leader, nationalized ITT's 70% interest in the Chilean Telephone Company (Chiltelco). ITT then proposed an 18-point action plan to the U.S. Government to strangle Chile's economy, create panic among its population, and cause social disorder, so the Chilean armed forces would overthrow Allende. Three months later President Nixon created a special inter-agency group to implement ITT's proposal, and the National Security Council's Committee approved a plan to oust Allende. ITT directors John A. McCone, former head of the CIA, and Eugene R. Black, former head of the World Bank, were instrumental in getting the U.S. to approve ITT's plan. Funding for the covert actions was channelled through the CIA, and the World Bank was one of the first financial institutions to cut off credit to Chile.

Allende was killed in 1973 in the resultant military coup funded by ITT, who were rewarded with the return of its holdings under new leader Augusto Pinochet's brutal dictatorship which saw thousands of Chileans tortured and murdered. Later in the decade, charges of perjury were brought against ITT for having denied involvement in the CIA-backed military coup to US Congress. ITT public relations officer Hal Hendrix pleaded guilty to lying under oath, but was fined under $100 as a reward for cooperation in the larger perjury case against ITT. The perjury case against ITT was dropped in 1979 on the grounds of 'international security', yet documents declassified in 2000 showed ITT to be guilty of perjury regarding its involvement in Chilean politics.

ITT & NIGERIA: ITT have also been accused of supporting corruption and meddling in politics in Nigeria throughout the 70's and 80's to protect their interests, whilst exploiting the country's wealth. Musician and activist Fela Kuti created the memorable song "ITT: International Thief Thief" as a comment on ITT's exploitation of Nigeria.

Despite its attempted re-branding, in 2007 ITT were found guilty of breaking US arms control laws by exporting secret night vision technology to foreign military and potential enemies of the US forces which led to the largest fine in history for breach of export control law. ITT paid a total monetary penalty of $100 million.

ITT is also the first major defence contractor convicted of a criminal violation of the Arms Export Control Act. ITT pleaded guilty to, between March 2001 and August 2001, exporting defense-related technical data to the People's Republic of China, Singapore, and the United Kingdom without having first obtained a license or written authorization from the U.S. Department of State. They also pleaded guilty to charges that, between April 2000 and October 2004, ITT Corporation left out material facts from Arms Exports Required Reports making the reports misleading. ITT admitted being aware that it was violating its export licenses and failing to stop the ongoing violations.

Ironically Forbes named ITT Corporation to its list of "America's Best Managed Companies" for 2008.

The Details Of The 'Decommissioners' Case & Verdict.

After the decommissioning, the 6 campaigners were arrested along with 2 others who were suspected of helping the decommissioners. As a result two of the defendants were held in remand in prison, one for 6 months, the other, Elijah Smith from Bristol, was held for 12 months.

Eventually in May 2010, the court case began, where 7 of the individuals were charged with 'conspiracy to commit criminal damage' by the prosecution. The activists faced the possibility of up to 8 years in jail if found guilty.

Although the activists admitted they had sabotaged the factory, their defence argued that criminal damage was legally justified if the damage occurs while trying to prevent greater damage to other properties - in this case, homes in Gaza. The lawful excuse defence was invoked, according to which it can be lawful to commit an offence to prevent a more serious crime.

In UK domestic law, the Rome Statute of the International Criminal Court applies, which makes it an offence for UK citizens and residents to act in complicity of war crimes that take place anywhere in the world. The defence stated that EDO MBM/ITT was acting unlawfully by assisting the crimes committed by the Israeli forces in Gaza at the same time as the SMASH EDO decommissioners destroyed manufacturing equipment. In this instance the defendants had to prove that not only were Israel committing war crimes at the exact time they enterred the factory, but also that when the action was taken they held a reasonable belief that the parts used in Israeli F16s were manufactured and exported from the Brighton factory.

EDO Managing director Paul Hills denied that the factory made the parts in question (VER-2 bomb racks and ERU-151 Ejector Release Units), but bemusingly brought in the very same trigger unit (as used exclusively by Israeli F16s) the next day to show the court, after he had denied that it was made in the factory. Paul Hills then changed his testimony claiming that they made parts for F16 fighters, but remained adamant that the components were not supplied to Israel and used in Gaza bombing raids.

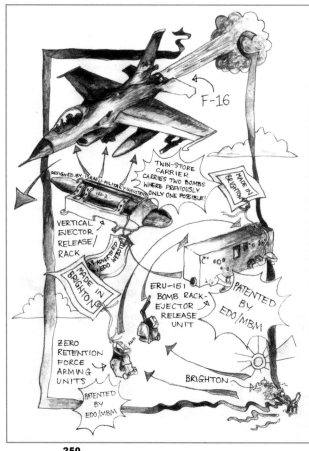

It came to light however, that the VER-2 bomb rack was a twin carrier bomb rack, whereas on all other non-Israeli F16's, only one bomb was possible per rack. The defence also obtained patents of EDO components, containing hebrew writing, and evidence was put to Hills about an illegal export of Beryllium to the US, to highlight that EDO had patented parts specifically for Israeli F16s, and were involved in illegal activities involving their exports.

After contradicting himself, the judge warned Paul Hills that he wasn't being asked about his activities, that illegal exports were criminal and he was under no obligation to admit a crime. Hills was also criticised for faxing the U.S. parent company EDO CORP (owned by ITT), as he was instruct-

WANTED

FOR COMPLICITY IN WAR CRIMES

PAUL HILLS: EDO/MBM (ITT SUBSIDUARY) MANAGING DIRECTOR

-ed not to contact third paries during the trial. Many of those following the case in court saw this action by Paul Hills as an attempt to cover his tracks and get his story straight.

As the Crown Court case continued, the judge and jury heard harrowing evidence from civilians who had been the targets of bombing by the Israeli Air-Force during the Gaza attacks and saw horrific evidence of war crimes. They also heard eye witness accounts provided by Sharyn Locke, an aid worker for ISM, who also had witnessed Israeli F16's bombing Gaza at the same time the decommissioning had taken place, including the use of white phospherous incendiary shells on civilian targets.

Caroline Lucas, MP for Brighton and the leader of the Green Party of England & Wales, supported the activists and said that this was a case in which she considered non-violent direct action legitimate.

Stephen Shay, prosecuting, argued that the factory was so small that even if it had been supplying Israel, it would have made no differen--ce to the war in Gaza.

The Judge summed up the two opposing arguments and implied that he disbelieved Paul Hills.

In his summing-up, George Bathurst-Norman suggested to the jury that "you may well think that hell on earth would not be an understatement of what the Gazans suffered in that time". The judge also highlighted the testimony by Green MP Caroline Lucas, that "all democratic paths had been exhausted" before the activists embarked on their action. "I am going to start with the background relating to Israel and Palestine and to the evidence which points to the war crimes being committed by Israel in Gaza, an area over which Israel has imposed a blockade."

"The evidence shows that those war crimes are committed against the civilian population of Gaza and against the property of its residents, including the United Nations by the Israeli Forces.

Commenting on Israeli's military operations in Gaza, Bathurst-Norman stated that: "Now you have to look at the evidence coldly and dispassionately. It may be as you went through what I can only describe as horrific scenes, scenes of devastation to civilian population, scenes which one would rather have hoped to have disappeared with the Nazi regimes of the last war, you may have felt anger and been absolutely appalled by them, but you must put that emotion aside."

Judge Bathurst-Norman also criticised the British and US governments, telling jurors: "You must put aside any feelings of being thoroughly ashamed of our government, of the American government and the United Nations and the EU in doing nothing about what was happening."

Christopher Osmond, 30, and Simon Levin, 35, both from Brighton, and Elijah Smith, 42, Tom Woodhead, 25, Ornella Saibene, 50, Bob Nicholls 52, and Harvey Tadman, 44, all from Bristol, were cleared of conspiracy to cause criminal damage.

This case represented a real 'David & Golliath' battle, providing a great victory and lawful justification for the anti-war protesters, who all walked free.

The Accustations & the Real Motivations for the Smash EDO Anti-war protesters.

After the verdict In late July 2010, Judge George Bathurst-Norman had become subject of a campaign of accusations by a number of right-wing columnists, the Zionist Federation, and the Board of Deputies of British Jews, claiming that his summary of the evidence was 'anti-semitic'. The Smash EDO campaigners were also accused of anti-semitism.

In response, the Smash EDO Campaign stated, "the charges of anti-semitism, which have been made against Bathurst-Norman, are a grossly cynical attempt to undermine the significance of these acquittals of the activists on evidence of Israeli war crimes. This evidence was not challenged by the Crown Prosecution Service. There is nothing anti-semitic in putting agreed evidence of Israeli war crimes to a jury."

The fact that the judge was advising the jury to look at the evidence coldly and dispassionately, to put opinions and political stances aside, seems not to register to the accusers. Nor did it seem to matter that many Smash EDO protesters and campaigners, including two of the defendants, are jewish, or of jewish descent.
Most disturbingly of all is the fact that these bodies seem unaware of, or in denial of ITT's direct and involved relationship with Nazi Germany, investing millions in, and building weapons for the nazi regime, even when the U.S. had gone to war, and the persecution of jewish people had become widespread throughout Europe. ITT supported the most devastatingly anti-semitic regime the world has known.

There is no denying it's very close relationship to other far-right dictators and their anti-semitic friends from Franco, right up through the 1970's to Augustus Pinochet. Pinochet too was a nazi sympathiser and collaborator, who protected the war criminal, nazi colonel, torturer and pedophile Paul Schaefer, who had fled to Chile prior to Pinochet's coup, to avoid a war crimes court. Pinochet supported Schaefer and allowed him to carry on with his nazi ideology; to create his own anti-semitic organisation within Chile, a colony which as well as running slave-labour camps (whilst paying no taxes), tortured communists and jews to death, up until the late 80's, whilst at the same time ITT was enjoying doing business throughout 'safe investment' Chile; the oppressive far-right regime it helped create. But where are the calls of anti-semitism towards ITT?

The fact that the Israeli government and it's political supporters turn a blind eye to ITT's anti-semitic and fascism-fuelled past, perhaps is telling of it's own selective denial of state oppression and war crimes it is party to. The reason given by the Israeli government to attack Gaza in 2008, was the 2,700 rocket and mortar attacks by jihadi and hamas from inside Gaza, aimed at Israeli settlements, and the 4 deaths and 75 injuries over a 2 year period. However, during that same period of 2005 to 2007, prior to the Gaza attacks, Israel fired more than 14,600 155mm artillery shells into the Gaza Strip, and committed many air strikes, killing 97 Gaza residents and injuring 298.

After the January 2008 gaza attacks had ended, the official figures said that approximately another 1400 people were killed, 431 of them were children. 15 hospitals were bombed, 40 clinics were heavily damaged or destroyed, 16 paramedics were killed, 22 injured. Over 50,000 Gaza residents were made homeless. Families having tea in their courtyards were attacked by bombers, women walking down the street with white flags looking for refuge from the attacks were also murdered. Israeli soldiers blindfolded and bound men and children and sent them out as human shields, a violation of International law.The Israeli gov-ernment have denied these claims even though there is much evidence, and claimed Hamas were responsible for war crimes.

A 575-page report by a fact-finding mission led by Justice Goldstone, organized by the U.N. Human Rights Council, called on both sides to thoroughly investigate the war crime allegations. Israel did not cooperate with the inv-

-estigation and judge Goldstone was branded an anti-semite, even though he criticised both sides. The fact-finding mission concluded that actions amounting to war crimes, and possibly in some respects crimes against humanity, were committed by the Israel Defense Forces. The report also said rockets fired by Palestinian militants into Israel where there were no military targets would also constitute war crimes, and perhaps crimes against humanity.

For those who value human life regardless of race or creed, the Gaza attacks represented a terrible chapter of murder & violence in the Israel - Palestine conflict. There is no denying to anyone who is a humanitarian and committed to peace, that the firing of rockets from inside Gaza against Israeli civilian settlements is a war crime and an act that terrorises families. I feel just as sad for the loss of life of Israeli civilians as I do for the loss of life of Palestinian civilians.

But there is no denying either, the difference between the proportionate damage and fatalities to Israeli settlements from rocket and mortar shells, compared to the death, destruction, and human rights abuses committed in the prison which is Gaza. The population is under a blockade, where food, medical supplies etc are below acceptable human rights standards, where the non-comb-atant civilian members of the population cannot leave. The residents of Gaza have suffered from the sustained might of Israeli military dominance, air strikes and artillery shellings on civilian targets over several years, this being just the latest saga in a struggle which has lasted decades, where Palestineans have continued to have lost land, homes, their rights and lives.

Groups such as 'The Parent Circle' and 'Combatants For Peace' made up of both Israelis and Palestineans who have either lost family members or have served in conflict, aim to bring both sides together and learn from the mistakes of the past. There is also the Israeli Committee Against House Demolitions (ICAHD) organisation, who are committed to ending the Israeli policy of demol-ishing Palestinean homes, and to finding peaceful solutions between the two nations. Another fairly recent example of people coming together were the non-violent protests at Budrus and Bil'in Where Palestinians and Israelis united to oppose the building of the Israeli West Bank Barrier through the town, which would have destroyed the Palestinian's olive groves, livelihood, and heritage. This was a peaceful victory which many see as a story of hope, of something to build upon. Many Israelis are now refusing military service, particularly in the Gaza strip, and are criticis-ing their own government. There is a huge difference between anti-semitism, and seeking to shut down, protest against and comment on those who are contributing to and enabling war crimes,who escalate conflict and the senseless loss of human life.

Likewise there is a growing number of British people who realise the hypocrisy of our own politic-ians talking 'peace', then protecting those british companies pro-fitting from making arms that kill civillians, and allowing them to hide details of what they are making and exporting, and where it is going, on the grounds that transparency 'might not be good for business'. I sincerely hope that the day comes where arms manufacture is not good for business.

It is only it seems, through the direct action of anti-war protesters like the Smash EDO campaign or the Raytheon 9 in Ireland, those who have exhausted all other means of stopping companies from literally 'getting away with murder', that we can truly fight for peace and change.The alternative insanity of keeping the cycle of wars, and death going so that companies can make a healthy profit, while continuing to influence government actions heavily doesn't bare thinking about.

Ornella Saibene, one of the acquitted defendants summed up the case in her own words; "We're very happy that a jury of ordinary people confronted with the facts recognised that our actions were justified... Presented what was going on in Palestine they have backed our action."

A SMASH EDO spokesperson, said "The government's spending review made only tiny cuts to the defence budget. Every job in the arms trade is still massively subsidised by the state. The exports made by EDO benefit only the CEOs. All this at the same time as the government is cutting the edu-cation and health budgets and hammering people's pensions and benefits. We say it's obvious where the budget cuts should be focused- on an arms trade that only benefits the corporations."

EDO/ ITT continues to trade in Brighton and to create arms components. The factory still do not admit that they make parts for the F16 Israeli bombers, despite the damning evidence. There has been no diclosed changes in it's policies.
SMASH EDO continue to campaign and demonstrate against the factory. To find out more about their campaign visit their website: http://www.smashedo.org.uk/

PARLIAMENTARY HYPOCRISY!
KIDS TODAY!
SNATCH!
I JUST DON'T UNDERSTAND!..
MADE IN UK
WHY THEY HAVEN'T LEARNED...
TO SETTLE DISPUTES...
WAR CHILD
WITHOUT RESORTING TO VIOLENCE!
I BLAME BAD PARENTS!

Campaign Against Arms Trade

Conflict

UK arms have been used by the Indonesian military in East Timor, Aceh and West Papua, by Zimbabwe in the Democratic Republic of Congo, by Argentina in the Falklands war, and by both sides in the Iran-Iraq war. The tension between India and Pakistan makes South Asia one of the most volatile regions of the world, yet the UK supplies arms to both countries.

Human Rights

Arms sales contribute to human rights abuses as they increase the military authority and capacity for abuses by governments. But two major markets for the UK are Saudi Arabia and Libya which rank as two of the most authoritarian regimes.

Development

Despite desperate poverty and its recent history of conflict, the UK Government is actively promoting arms exports to Angola. In 2008, it organised an 'industry day' where HMS Liverpool docked in Angolan waters and hosted Angolan political and military officials.

The policy and practice of selling arms

Government rhetoric speaks of arms control, but its policy and practice is to promote arms sales with little or no regard for the damage they might cause. Most countries where major conflicts are taking place are recipients of UK arms. Human rights abusing governments and authoritarian regimes rank among the UK's most important markets. Development concerns are irrelevant as long as a country is willing to pay for weaponry.

CAAT supporters protest at BAE's AGM after investigations into the arms company were ended.

The Government's arms sales unit

Arms receive official assistance far in excess of other industrial sectors, and from several UK Government departments. The most obvious manifestation of this support is the arms sales unit - the Defence & Security Organisation - within UK Trade & Investment (UKTI DSO). This unit has 180 staff dedicated to arms sales. The specific suppor provided to ALL non-arms sectors amounts to 142 staff. Arms sales account for 56% of sector specific staff resources despite arms being only 1.5% of total exports.

The case for ending arms export promotion

The UK is one of the main players in the destructive international arms trade. Farm from seeking to control or restrain arms sales, the Government actively promotes them, dedicating resources to arms sales promotion far beyond that available to other industries.

If arms export promotion across Government departments was to end, the most immediate result would be that the Government 's own arms export guidelines could be meaningfully implemented and the worst of UK arms sales could be stopped.

Security is being threatened and economic opportunities missed because of the prioritisation of the private internatuional arms company interests over those of the UK public. A significant first step towards correcting the imbalance would be to end the Government's extensive arms selling activities and shut UKTI DSO.

Campaign Against Arms Trade is working to end government support for the arms trade. CAAT helped to shut down the government's previous, larger arms promotiond department, and forced a multinational company to pull out of holding the world's largest arms fair in London.

Support Campaign Against Arms Trade

You can support Campaign Against Arms Trade by getting involved with the campaign or donating.

Details of how to get involved, and more information can be found on CAAT's website:
www.caat.org.uk